ARCHITECTURAL TREASURES OF EARLY AMERICA

★ ★ ★ ★ ★ ★ ★ ★

SURVEY
OF
EARLY AMERICAN DESIGN

ARCHITECTURAL TREASURES OF EARLY AMERICA

SURVEY
OF
EARLY AMERICAN DESIGN

From material originally published as
The White Pine Series of Architectural Monographs
edited by
Russell F. Whitehead and Frank Chouteau Brown

Prepared for this series by the staff of
The Early American Society

Robert G. Miner, Editor
Anne Annibali, Design and Production
Jeff Byers, Design and Production
Nancy Dix, Editorial Assistant
Patricia Faust, Editorial Assistant
Carol Robertson, Editorial Assistant

An
Early
American
Society
Book

Published by Arno Press Inc.

Copyright © 1977 by Arno Press Inc. and The Early American Society, Inc.

Library of Congress Cataloging in Publication Data

Main entry under title:

Survey of Early American design.

(Architectural treasures of early America ; v. 8)
(An Early American Society book)
Includes index.
1. Architecture, Colonial—United States.
2. Architecture—United States. 3. Architecture—
Details. I. Miner, Robert G. II. Early American
Society. III. The Monograph series, records of early
American architecture. IV. Series.
NA707.S94   720'.974   77-14468

ISBN: 0-405-10071-X (Arno)   ISBN: 0-517-53273-5 (Crown)
Distributed to the book trade by Crown Publishers, Inc.

CONTENTS

Detail "A"

Detail "B"

6"x6" POST.
2"x4" STODS.
6"x10" GIRDER
7/8"x2" FURRING STRIPS.
FINISHED FLOOR
1x3 BR...
ROUGH FLOOR
...ALSAM WOOL
BRICK FIRE STOP
PLASTER CEILING
DRAWN - Ke...

Lower Delaware Valley

THE Massachusetts colonist disregarded the abundant supply of stone about him and built a timber house. The early Pennsylvania colonist, hailing from a different part of England, settled in a land heavily wooded with a plentiful supply of the best timber heart could wish and used it merely to construct a log cabin for temporary shelter until he had time to quarry stone or bake bricks and build a dwelling of a type like that to which he had been accustomed in the Mother Country. If one may be permitted the indulgence of making a very bromidic observation, we are all creatures of habit. In no one particular is our addiction to hereditary custom more likely to come to the surface than in matters of architecture. This tendency on the part of the first settlers to stick to their own several architectural traditions has been pointed out more than once.

Although the persistent ignoring of physical conditions and clinging to traditional preference for materials and methods of construction, which the colonists, their·fathers, and their grandfathers before them had been used to in England, gave the domestic architecture of our earliest Colonial period both variety and a pronounced individual bias, according to the town or shire the settlers had come from, common sense and necessity in time brought modifications, while independence of action and originality grew apace. Independent action, however, in the face of customary usage was always somewhat of an exception; and as exceptions are generally of special interest, for their comparative rarity if for no other reason, so we find it in the case of the wooden houses of Eastern Pennsylvania, West Jersey and Delaware, a portion of the land where the majority of the English settlers showed their traditional preference for stone or brick.

The Swedes in Delaware apparently had no predisposition against timber and used it. Among the colonists of British origin, the men of West Jersey, notwithstanding the excellent early brickwork there to be seen, were the first to adapt themselves to conditions with good grace, make a virtue of necessity, and build of timber when it was well-nigh impossible to get stone and nearly as difficult to come by suitable brick. Their soil was stoneless, good brick clay was scarce, the pine growth was abundant, and they did the obvious thing—they built of timber. And posterity has never had cause to regret their choice. In Pennsylvania wooden structures of any amenity came later—the end of the eighteenth century and the early part of the nineteenth—and reflected the characteristics of the time. In each of these three States, the domestic wooden architecture has peculiarities of its own, but all of it yields interest and from all of it something suitable for modern adaptation can be gained.

In Delaware, at a very early date, dwellings of the type of the oldest house in Dover—chosen as an illustration, not for appearances, but for its archæological value—were not uncommon and were also to be seen in the Swedish portions of Philadelphia. They were of mixed English and Swedish parentage. The outstanding chimney is English, the gambrel roof with its sharp lower pitch sounds a Scandinavian note in contour. The type is simple but strong, and susceptible of interesting development. The old batten shutters, with boards set chevron-wise to form a her-

HOUSE AT GREENWICH, NEW JERSEY.

ring-bone figure, still left on one of the lower windows, are to be noted as characteristic of this part of the country. Despite the neglect and ill usage to which this house has plainly been subjected, its clapboard walls and shingle roof are still staunch and weather-worthy.

Across the Delaware River, in South and West Jersey, where the easy and substantial affluence of a fertile farming region of large plantations encouraged building, one finds a different condition obtaining. From Salem up to Burlington or Bordentown, in the face of stone and brick tradition and the precedent of numerous fine examples of early brickwork, especially in the neighborhood of Salem, many of the prosperous farmers soon took to the course of least resistance and built of wood.

One of the first, and one of the most interest-

OLDEST HOUSE AT DOVER, DELAWARE.

ing, examples of West Jersey wooden architecture is "The Willows," on a point of land jutting into Newton Creek near Gloucester, a structure dating from about 1720. It was once a handsome country seat, but, years ago, owing to the encroachment of manufacturing plants, became untenable as a residence and was abandoned to tenancy and truck-farming. Nevertheless, despite its external dilapidation and sorry surroundings, the house presents features that the student of architecture cannot afford to neglect. Indeed, just because of its dilapidation, some of its structural peculiarities have become visible and admit of easy analysis in a way that would be impossible in a structure kept in decent repair. Besides being one of the earliest wooden houses, it shows the combination of a later addi-

"THE WILLOWS," GLOUCESTER, NEW JERSEY.
Built circa 1720.

THE EWING HOUSE, MOORESTOWN, NEW JERSEY. Built circa 1800.

tion, with its opportunity for making comparisons, not to be found in any other of the contemporary buildings in the neighborhood. The older or eastern portion (to the right in the picture) is built of three-inch white pine planks, double grooved with sliding tongues and even joints dovetailed together at the corners. The structure is really a piece of cabinet work rather than a piece of carpentry, and is a monument to the skill of the joiner—the old term is peculiarly appropriate for the artisan in this instance—who framed it together. It is only since the loosening and dropping off of the corner boards that this feature of construction has become visible.

"The Willows," as are also nearly all other old West Jersey wooden houses, is "brick-paned," or lined with a solid brick wall inside the plank or clapboard exterior and between the studs. So substantial is the structure and so thorough the workmanship, that, after nearly two centuries, only slight repairs and reasonable care are needed to make it as fit as it ever was.

Of an entirely different type are the capacious, foursquare, clapboarded houses, of slightly later date, that are to be found a-plenty throughout West Jersey. Of this class the house at Bordentown may be regarded as representative, or the house at Salem. These houses boasted a symmetrical, rectangular plan with central hallway from front to back,—rooms on each side of it, an ell extension at the rear, and chimneys at each gabled end. There is rarely any attempt at embellishment, for most of these houses were built by plain Friends who had conscientious objections both to collars on their coats and ornament on their dwellings. The simplest kind of cornice is ordinarily the only concession to the impulse for decoration. Otherwise, nine out of every ten are as plain as the proverbial pipestem, but their proportions are usually agreeable and their general aspect seems to fit in with the quiet affluence and unassuming thrift that furnishes forth their old mahogany midday dinner table with blue Canton and old silver and yet

HOUSE NEAR PHILADELPHIA, PENNSYLVANIA.

HOUSE AT BORDENTOWN, NEW JERSEY. Doorway Detail.

sets master in shirt sleeves and men in overalls side by side to devour the plenteous fare.

Of more urbane and polished type by far, is the Haddonfield house that appears in the illustration. Chronologically characteristic of the early nineteenth century, it also combines in its aspect an unmistakable note of Quaker reticence and austerity. The usual Classic Revival type is perfectly familiar, but here is a Classic Revival type pared down, attenuated, robbed of all self-assertion, and compressed into Quaker simplicity. The residuum from the transformation turns out to be singularly agreeable. The house,

with a door at one side of the front, two windows beside it, three windows on the front of the second floor, and a wing or extension at the side or the rear, belongs to a well recognized type that flourished at the beginning of the nineteenth century. But this type commonly exhibited an accompaniment of some emphatic Classic details. Here, on the contrary, we have the Classic items reduced to the lowest terms, like a rigid Quaker's speech and fashion of garb, and with some elegance withal. Had any more been subtracted, there would have been a risk of meriting the shrewd old countryman's criticism, upon seeing

HOUSE AT BORDENTOWN, NEW JERSEY.
Built circa 1740.

17 Market Street. **SALEM, NEW JERSEY.**

a new building of exceedingly restrained and austere design: "That ain't no architecture; that's a packing box."

Of great charm is the house on the Haddonfield Pike, set amid its box bushes and ancient yew trees, with its modest porches and its side wing expanded into a broad gambrel-roofed structure, only a little less in size than the main body of the dwelling. The house is thoroughly representative of the town, which is itself representative of the best traditions of West Jersey wooden architecture, peculiarly reminiscent of Elizabeth Haddon, that firm and virile-minded seventeenth-century maiden who assumed her father's interests, founded the town, courted and married—of her own initiative, tradition says—and continued to sign and be known by her maiden name.

Another house typical of West Jersey domestic architecture in wood, the previously mentioned eighteenth-century building at Bordentown, might be called the decorated member of the symmetrically arranged rectangular dwelling class. The detail of the Bordentown building (1740) is rather unique in point of the course of small panels below a frieze ornamented with drapery swags, the fine mouldings of the window casings, and the slender, semi-engaged pillars of the door frame that suggest the work of an artisan from the Dutch counties of North Jersey.

A reversion to the old type of smooth-jointed, grooved-plank construction may be seen in the Moorestown house, dating from about 1800. Both in plan and architectural amenity the illustrations show this building is a highly creditable exemplar of what may be achieved in a wooden medium.

HOUSE AT WOODSTOWN, NEW JERSEY.

The Bilderbeck House. **SALEM, NEW JERSEY.**

The Bilderbeck House. **SALEM, NEW JERSEY.**

These several types of West and South Jersey wooden houses have set a precedent that has been assiduously followed by later generations in New Jersey towns, so far as material alone is concerned. How much better they might have followed or adapted it in the matter of architectural expression, the "man who was blind in one eye and couldn't see with the other" might tell at a glance. One needs only go through the coast towns or the inland Jersey towns but a little way from New York to be overpowered with the dreary horrors perpetrated anywhere between 1860 and 1885, or even later. Between those years the jig-saw decorator was rampaging at large and embellishing (?) the wooden packing boxes that prostituted a noble building material and did more to give wood, for the time being, a bad name as an architectural medium than any other one thing in the history of building. The old houses show what charm frame dwellings were capable of presenting in intelligent hands.

The wooden architecture of the Lower Delaware Valley, while not so abundant as in some other parts of the country, for reasons already mentioned, is nevertheless invested with the merit of a distinct individuality, or several individualities, and has its share to contribute both to the story of house building in America and to modern inspiration.

THE BILDERBECK HOUSE, SALEM, NEW JERSEY. Built in 1813.

HOUSE AT HADDONFIELD, NEW JERSEY.
Built circa 1810.

HOUSE AT 17 MARKET STREET, SALEM, NEW JERSEY.

THE PRICE HOUSE, GERMANTOWN, PENNSYLVANIA.

THE OLD MORAVIAN SEMINARY—"BELL HOUSE"—BETHLEHEM, PENNSYLVANIA
Built during 1745-1746

Bethlehem, Pennsylvania

THE colonial domain in America comprised regions which differed conspicuously from one another in climate, soil, and economic opportunity. The races which came to dwell in these new lands were no less diverse than the country.

By 1763, the total white population of the region from Maine to Georgia was not far from 1,250,000. It has been estimated that more than one-third of the inhabitants were newcomers, not of the stock of the original settlers. These newcomers were chiefly French, German, and Scotch-Irish, but their influence on colonial life was less than their numbers might suggest. The Germans, as farmers, contributed greatly to the prosperity of the communities where they cultivated their lands.

Pennsylvania, the last of the colonies to be founded, except Georgia, contained a kaleidoscopic collection of people of different bloods and religions. The population increased from 50,000 in 1730 to more than 200,000 in 1763 due, in the largest part, to the thousands of Scotch-Irish and Germans, who poured into the colony, The Scotch-Irish went to the region of the Susquehanna. The Germans usually settled near the old counties, where they could devote themselves to the cultivation of the soil, and to the maintenance of their many peculiarities of life and faith. The life of these Germans-Moravians, Mennonites, Schwenkfelders, Dunkards, and many, many others, was marked by simplicity, docility, mystical faith, and rigid economy. The Germans were unaccustomed to liberty of thought as to political liberty, and it produced a new sect or religious distinction almost every day. Some of them were inclined to monastic and hermit life.

Most of the German sects left the Quakers in undisturbed possession of Philadelphia, and spread out into the surrounding region which was then a wilderness. They settled in a half circle beginning at Easton-on-the-Delaware passing up the Lehigh Valley into Lancaster County and down the Susquehanna.

The Moravians are a Christian sect founded by disciples of John Huss during the 15th Century in Moravia, a former province in the northwest of Austria-Hungary, and now included in Czecho-Slovakia. The sect is also known as the United Brethren or Unity of Brethren. The Moravians, under the patronage of Count Zinzendorf, were constantly seeking a wider field for their missionary work, and we find that as early as 1727 Count Zinzendorf, who later became the leading bishop of the Moravian Church, purchased a tract of land in the province of Georgia for a colony of Schwenkfeldian exiles from Silesia. It was not until the spring of 1735, however, that the Moravians made their settlement in Georgia, and brought the gospel to the Indians and the negro slaves. A school for Indian children was established on the Savannah River, a mile above the town of Savannah. The war between England and Spain, which occurred a few years after the settlement in Georgia, interfered with the work of the missionaries, so that in 1740 they decided to move their activities to Pennsylvania where they could be among the German Colonists, and administer to the spiritual welfare of the Indians in that region. It is interesting to note that the Indians near Bethlehem, who had been converted to Christianity by the Moravians were the only ones who did not follow Pontiac when in 1763 the tribes swept eastward into Pennsylvania, burning, murdering, leveling every habitation to the ground.

In the "Forks of the Delaware" they purchased five thousand acres of land, and at Nazareth in May, 1740, founded their first settlement in Pennsylvania, under the leadership of Rev. George Whitefield. The first house that was built is now called the "Grey House." It is a log house constructed of hewn white oak.

The most imposing building erected by the Moravians at Nazareth was intended originally to be the manor house for Count Zinzendorf. The style and construction are typical of Moravian colonial architecture. The builders evidently were striving to create the domestic atmosphere of the houses in Silesia in order to make Count Zinzendorf feel at home in the new country. The corner-stone was laid in 1755 and the structure completed in 1759. The building was never

THE STEUBEN HOUSE, REPUBLIC HILL, PENNSYLVANIA

THE SHIMER FARM HOUSE, BUILT 1801, NEAR BETHLEHEM, PENNSYLVANIA

occupied as a residence, but was formally opened in 1759 as the Boys' School of the American Province of the Church. The cupola was added in 1785.

The main body of the Moravians did not remain long in Nazareth, due to differences between Rev. Whitefield and his followers. They decided to purchase five hundred acres of land which lay at the junction of the Lehigh River and the Monocacy Creek. Here they were reinforced by colonists who had come to the "back country" from Germantown, Pennsylvania, and a new settlement was established. They built their first log house in December, 1740, in what is now the thriving industrial city of Bethlehem. It was Count Zinzendorf who, stimulated by the associations connected with the celebration of Christmas, gave the place its Biblical name.

Of the several Moravian buildings at Bethlehem which remain in but slightly altered condition, the ⊔-shaped group made up of the "Brother's House," the "Sisters' Home," and the Seminary are the most exotic, and show a well-defined architecture of German derivation. We are reminded, by the heavy stone and timber construction, the steep roofs with two rows of sloping dormers, and the flanking buttresses, of the medieval buildings of the old world.

THE "GREY HOUSE", NAZARETH, PENNSYLVANIA
The first Moravian house in Pennsylvania

The left wing of the group is the second house that was built in Bethlehem. During the first years of the settlement, "The House on the Lehigh" served as a home and hospice, manse and church, administration office, academy, dispensary and town hall; the loved resting place of weary pilgrims, the busiest center to be found far and wide, sought out by the inquisitive and expatiated on by many a gossip, who told wonderful stories about the Moravians. The building was called "*Gemeinhaus*" in the German nomenclature or community house. It stands today in its original form although its massive logs are hidden by clapboards.

The middle building of the group, the "Bell House," is officially known as "the old Seminary" among the Moravian properties because the boarding school for girls occupied it from 1749 to 1790. It was built originally to contain the refectory of the single men, a general dining room connected with the Community House, and the quarters for the married people. The foundation lines were staked off, August 24, 1745, but the building was not completed until October of the following year. The bell turret, which was to contain the first town clock, was erected in June, 1746. Augustine Neisser of Germantown, began work on the clock in April, 1746, but did not complete it until February 15, 1747. The three bells, one large and two smaller ones, were cast by Samuel Powell, who was also the first innkeeper on the south side of Bethlehem. The weather vane, which still surmounts the little turret was made from a drawing by Cammerhoff. The historic emblem of the Church, a lamb with a banner, is part of the design.

The Moravian "Sisters' House" forms the right wing of this group. The designers appear to have harked back to the Gothic architecture of the smaller German towns with which they were familiar. They seem to have felt the need of the huge buttresses even though there are no vaults or cross arches to sustain.

The court yard, or open square formed by the three buildings, was long the scene of Holy-Day musicals, and Harvest-home festivals.

THE MORAVIAN "SISTERS HOUSE"—BETHLEHEM, PENNSYLVANIA

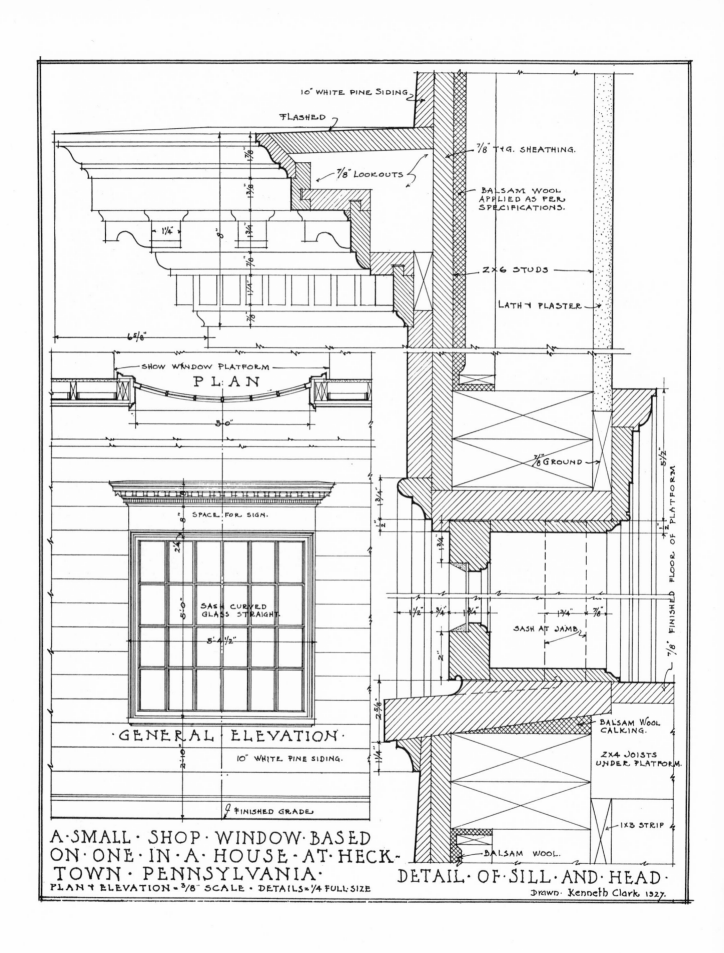

10" WHITE PINE SIDING.

FLASHED

7/8" LOOKOUTS

7/8" T&G. SHEATHING.

BALSAM WOOL APPLIED AS PER SPECIFICATIONS.

2×6 STUDS

LATH & PLASTER

SHOW WINDOW PLATFORM

P L A N

3'-0"

6 5/8"

7/8 GROUND

SPACE FOR SIGN.

SASH CURVED
GLASS STRAIGHT.

5'-4 1/2"

SASH AT JAMB

7/8 FINISHED FLOOR OF PLATFORM

·GENERAL ELEVATION·

10" WHITE PINE SIDING.

BALSAM WOOL CALKING.

2×4 JOISTS UNDER PLATFORM.

1×3 STRIP

BALSAM WOOL.

FINISHED GRADE

A·SMALL·SHOP·WINDOW·BASED
ON·ONE·IN·A·HOUSE·AT·HECK-
TOWN·PENNSYLVANIA·
PLAN & ELEVATION = 3/8" SCALE · DETAILS = 1/4 FULL SIZE

·DETAIL·OF·SILL·AND·HEAD·
Drawn. Kenneth Clark 1927.

Window Detail
THE SHIMER HOUSE, NEAR BETHLEHEM, PA.

The region around Bethlehem is dotted with the typical unpretentious Pennsylvania "farm houses," the original dwellings of Moravian farmers. The outside walls are of stone with gables at the lateral ends. It will be noted that the windows have fifteen lights, nine in the upper sash and six in the lower. The Steuben House at Republic Hill is one of the exceptions to the usual spacing of two windows on each side of the door opening. Panelled shutters, exposing a plain flush surface, on the outside when closed, and the panels on the inside when opened, are typical. In the examples illustrated, the rail between the two large panels seem arranged so as to continue the line of the meeting rail of the window.

The measured drawings of the doorway of the Freeman house in Freemansburg, about two miles from Bethlehem, show an important piece of work, important because it contains some odd twists to well known architectural motives. The tulip decoration recalls the Pennsylvania Dutch painted furniture, but the cornice, frieze, entablature, and columns were not taken out of the "Books" or *Builders' Assistants.*

The term "Pennsylvania Dutch," used in speaking about the eighteenth century buildings in Pennsylvania, has come to mean German and Swedish, more often than Netherlandish. It was the German frontiersmen who played the largest part in the "back country" around Bethlehem, and their influence on the adopted style of building has given the domestic architecture of the state an air of its own, quite different from that found in the other colonies. The feeling that pervades the old farmhouses has been so imbided and availed of by modern architects that there are many thousand just such houses everywhere throughout this territory and it is difficult for the traveler to believe in the real antiquity of some of the old houses, their flavor is so very modern.

In these days of cold facts, commercialism, and expensive frontages, one feels that Art is being shoved into the discard, and when a good old building is demolished to make room for an "Ultra Modern" duplex apartment house, one knows that the Goddess of Beauty is getting an awfully raw deal. It is remarkable and commendable, that the Moravians in Bethlehem, have preserved, practically without an alteration, their group of institutional buildings in the heart of an industrial city.

Detail of Stone Wall
THE STEUBEN HOUSE, REPUBLIC HILL, PA.

MANOR HOUSE FOR COUNT ZINZENDORF, NAZARETH, PENNSYLVANIA
Opened in 1759 as The Boys' School of the American Province of the Church

THE ROHN FARM HOUSE, BATH VILLAGE NEAR BETHLEHEM, PENNSYLVANIA

THE SHIMER FARM HOUSE—ALONG LEHIGH RIVER NEAR BETHLEHEM, PA.

DOORWAY—HOUSE ON MINSI TRAIL, BETHLEHEM, PENNSYLVANIA

The JOHN FREEMAN HOUSE
FREEMANSBURG, PENNSYLVANIA

DRAWINGS *from The George F. Lindsay Collection*

DETAIL OF MAIN ENTRANCE

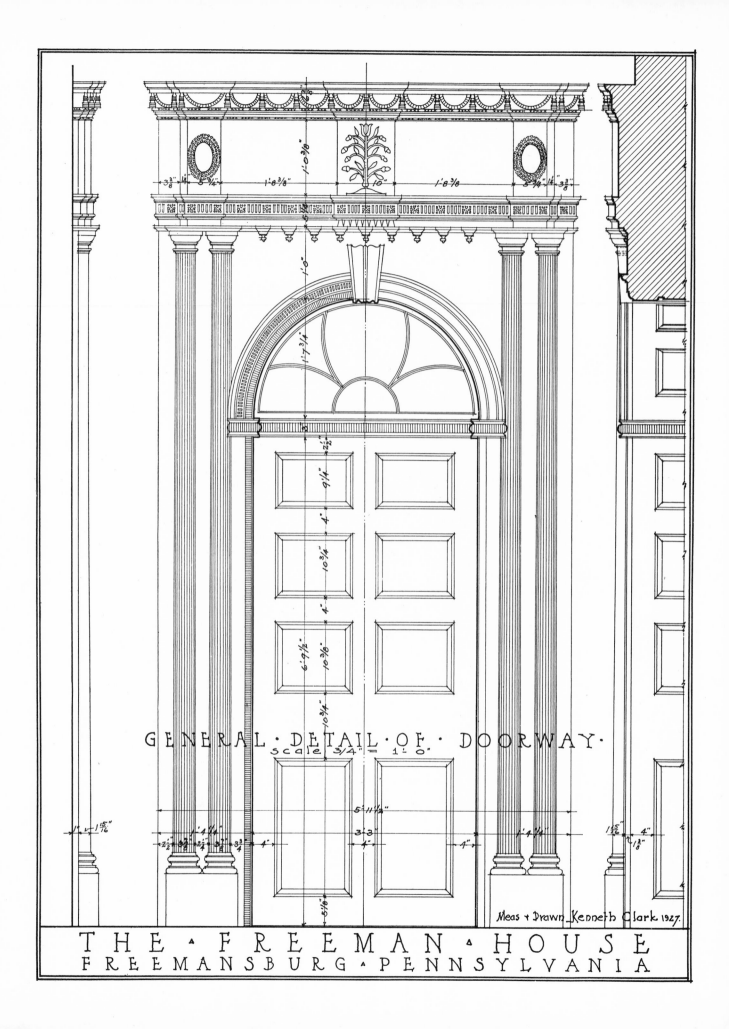

GENERAL · DETAIL · OF · DOORWAY ·
scale 3/4" = 1'·0"

Meas + Drawn Kenneth Clark 1927.

THE · FREEMAN · HOUSE
FREEMANSBURG · PENNSYLVANIA

DOORWAY—THE JOHN FREEMAN HOUSE, FREEMANSBURG, PENNSYLVANIA

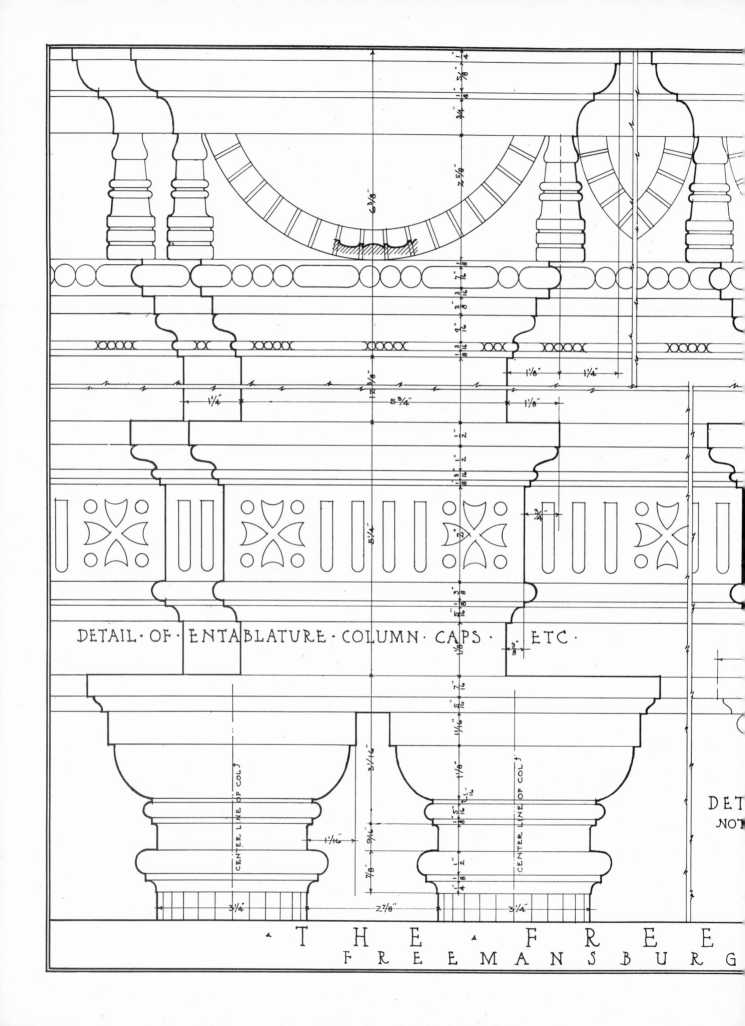

DETAIL · OF · ENTABLATURE · COLUMN · CAPS · ETC ·

· T H E · F R E E
F R E E M A N S B U R G

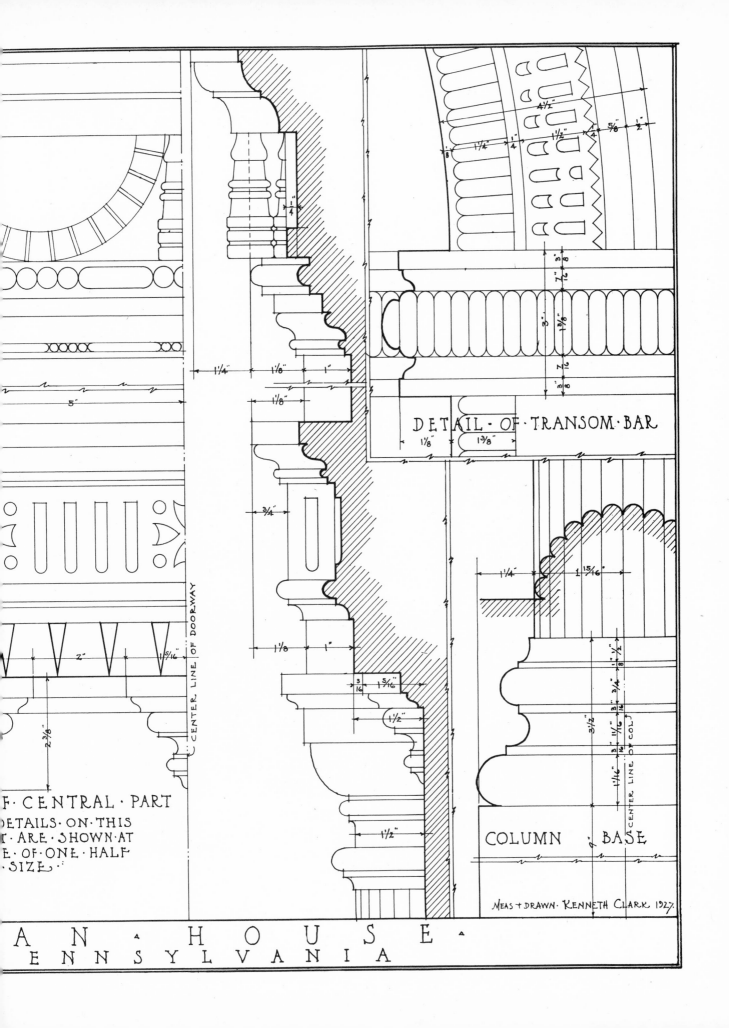

DETAIL · OF · TRANSOM · BAR

CENTER · LINE · OF · DOORWAY

F · CENTRAL · PART
DETAILS · ON · THIS
· ARE · SHOWN · AT
· OF · ONE · HALF
· SIZE ·

COLUMN · BASE

CENTER · LINE · OF · COL.

MEAS + DRAWN · KENNETH CLARK 1927.

AN · HOUSE ·
ENNSYLVANIA

CUPOLA OF THE MORAVIAN BOYS' SCHOOL—"NAZARETH HALL", NAZARETH, PA.
Built in 1785

CUPOLA—THE MORAVIAN CHURCH, BETHLEHEM, PENNSYLVANIA
Built in 1803

Doorway Detail

THE HUNTER HOUSE, NEAR YELLOW HOUSE, PENNSYLVANIA

Berks County Farmhouses

THE fertile limestone Valley of Oley in the County of Berks, Pennsylvania, furnishes us with a valuable architectural heritage. The area of the valley consists of some thirty square miles and is situated near Reading in the eastern portion of the county as may be seen in the accompanying map. In Friedensburg (Oley), Pleasantville, Lime Kiln, Spangsville, and Yellow House we find excellent examples of century old farmhouses which contribute much to our understanding of the homes of our ancestors and to the records of early American architecture.

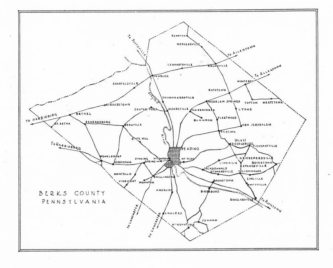

BERKS COUNTY
PENNSYLVANIA

The settlers who arrived during the latter part of the seventeenth and the early eighteenth centuries were chiefly French Huguenot refugees, fleeing from their native country to escape the persecutions of the times and coming in search of religious freedom in a place where they could make their new homes.

William Penn, when first laying out his colony in 1682, divided it into three counties, Philadelphia, Chester, and Bucks, all radiating from a point where the city of Philadelphia now stands. Naturally, the first settlers followed the water courses to their best advantage. The Swedes, coming up the Schuylkill River, settled above the mouth of the Monocacy Creek, where the town of Douglassville is now located. There today may be found some of the earliest signs of civilized life in the County, and a few of the early houses, including the Mounce Jones House, erected in 1716, which is perhaps the oldest house still standing in what is now Berks County.

Following the Swedes, the English Quakers, coming up the Manatawny Creek, located in the present Oley, along with a number of French and Swiss Huguenots, as well as German families. Such Huguenot names as DeTurk, De LaVan, De LaPlank, Bertelot, DeLong, as well as others have survived from the earliest

settlement to the present time.

In 1698, John Keim, a young German, was the first known settler to stake and lay claim to a tract of land in Oley. In 1706, returning from Europe with his bride, he began to clear his land for cultivation and later erected a stone dwelling, which is still standing. In 1712, Isaac DeTurck, a brother-in-law of Keim, coming from New York, settled on a tract near the present village of Friedensburg.

Between this time and 1720 other French Huguenots, as well as the Lees, English Quakers, headed by Anthony Lee, the first to arrive in Oley, in 1718 settled in what is now known as the village of Pleasantville. The Lees were soon joined by the Boone family and others of the same religion, and as early as 1726 they had organized themselves into a separate congregation and built their first church of logs. In 1736 it is known that George Boone collected funds for a larger and better structure. Later this also was found to be insufficient, and the third, the present Exeter Friends' Meeting House, was built sometime before 1800, the exact date is unknown. It is one of the oldest Quaker Meeting Houses in Pennsylvania, outside of Philadelphia.

In the possession of Daniel Fisher, present owner, and great-grandson of Henry Fisher, the builder of the Fisher Homestead near Yellow House, there is a brief of title stating that on April 20, 1682, during the reign of King Charles II, William Penn, of Worminghurst, Sussex County, England, deeded to John Sheiras of York County, England, 1,000 acres of land in the Province of Pennsylvania. The land changed hands several times until, in 1791, John Lesher sold some three hundred acres to Henry Fisher, showing that a large part of the land must have been sold off before this time. The buildings on the

37

THE SPANG HOUSE, SPANGSVILLE, PENNSYLVANIA

THE HUNTER HOUSE, NEAR YELLOW HOUSE, PENNSYLVANIA

EXETER FRIENDS' MEETING HOUSE, NEAR STONERSVILLE, PENNSYLVANIA

land were already old and as soon as it could be arranged, preparations were made for building a new house, which was finished in 1801. Nearby stands a large spring house in which, no doubt, the family lived while the house was being erected.

The Kaufman House, is one of the original houses in the Valley although larger than the majority. This house, like so many others in the neighborhood, is now used as an outbuilding for the new house which was built when larger quarters were needed. These first houses are sturdy old places of stone and timber, entirely lacking in embellishment but beautiful in their proportions. Often built into the slope of a hill near or directly over a spring, the houses thereby served the double purpose of dwelling and spring house. The plan is usually rectangular with but one or two main rooms on each floor. The kitchen is on the lower floor, in cases where the house was built into a hill. Here one may see the huge fireplace with smoked hewn timber lintel and simple board mantel shelf.

The Fisher House, today, is perhaps the best preserved in the Oley Valley, outside of some that have been restored, and may well be considered typical of

the Pennsylvania farmhouse. The exterior walls are of limestone, as are the majority of the dwellings of this type. There is a pedimented doorway at the center of the broad front of the main rectangle, opening into a spacious hallway, dividing the large rooms devoted to living and dining purposes. The kitchen is in a wing which projects from the main house. This addition is also built of rough stone but the original detail has been modified.

The flat arch above the window openings deserves mention, because a similar form of stone arch frequently occurs in houses throughout Pennsylvania. Here in the Fisher House a flat arch is fashioned of wood, with a central key block of greater height than the adjoining pieces. The cornice mouldings and doorway detail seem to be identical with many of the other houses and it is interesting to note how the modification of the same detail has been used on the main cornice, the pedimented doorway, the mantels, and the cornices of rooms and hallways. The detail may have been original with the builder or more probably copied from some carpenter's manual so much in use at that time. The chief carpenter of the Fisher House is known to have been Gottlieb Drexel, and to him belongs the credit of the fine paneling, stairway, friezes, cornices, and other architectural features.

The house contains six fireplaces, some of which are faced on the outside with Italian marble and plastered on the inside. Possibly the most beautiful of these, and the most intricate in its detail, is the one in the bridal chamber or guest room.

The George Boone House, erected in 1733, with its whitewashed stone walls, is interesting in its spacing of windows on the front wall and the lack of windows and the mere slits which occur on the end walls. A line of timber may be seen projecting on the end walls, as if to form the gable end but on further thought the wall was moved back some few feet. Evidently the wall was never terminated to form this gable as no distinct jointing can be seen where the new wall would have joined the old, and the date 1733 scratched into one of the sandstone quoins of the rear wall leads one to believe this was the original wall. However, the difference in the pitch of the two roofs gives anything but a pleasing proportion. It is said that George Boone, the grandfather of Daniel Boone, was well content to live in his simple log cabin nearby until his death in 1744, declaring the new home was much too pretentious for his simple tastes. It was actually occupied by his eldest son, George Boone, II.

It is an interesting fact that these early homesteads, found within a radius of a few miles, have remained in the possession of descendants for the past century.

Much could and has been said of the picturesque outbuildings, the spring and tenant houses, bake ovens and smoke houses spotting the Oley countryside, with their whitewashed or plastered stone walls, and many still retaining their weathered red tile roofs. All of these, worked out and planned to the best advantage, together with the well built farmhouses, speak loudly of the thrift, domestic loyalty, and good taste of these early immigrants.

THE GEORGE BOONE HOUSE, NEAR LIME KILN, PENNSYLVANIA

THE FISHER HOUSE, NEAR YELLOW HOUSE, PENNSYLVANIA

First Floor Hallway
THE FISHER HOUSE, NEAR YELLOW HOUSE, PENNSYLVANIA

THE FISHER HOUSE, NEAR YELLOW HOUSE, PENNSYLVANIA

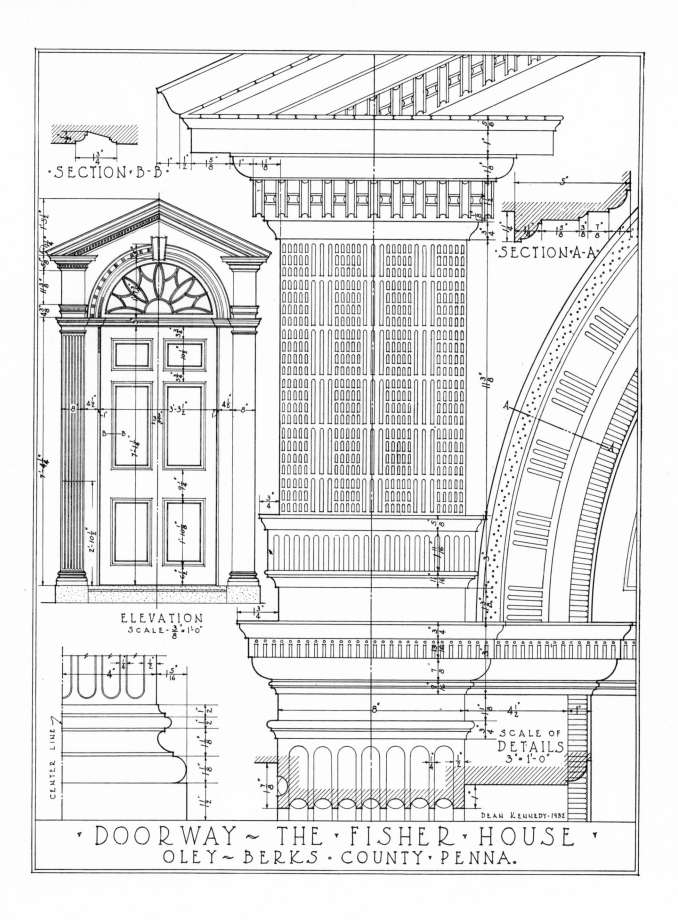

·SECTION·B-B·

·SECTION·A-A·

ELEVATION
SCALE- $\frac{3}{8}$"=1'-0"

CENTER LINE

SCALE OF
DETAILS
3"=1'-0"

DEAN KENNEDY·1932

·DOORWAY ~ THE·FISHER·HOUSE·
OLEY ~ BERKS·COUNTY·PENNA.

BRIDAL CHAMBER—THE FISHER HOUSE, NEAR YELLOW HOUSE, PENNSYLVANIA

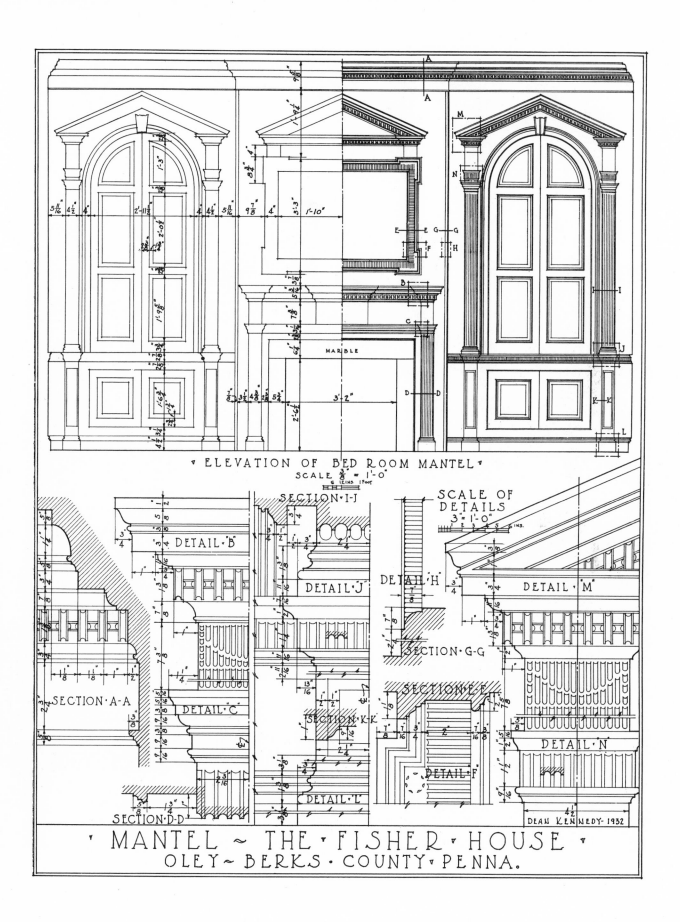

▿ ELEVATION OF BED ROOM MANTEL ▿
SCALE ⅜" = 1'-0"

MARBLE

DETAIL·B

SECTION·I-J

SCALE OF DETAILS
3" = 1'-0"

DETAIL·H

DETAIL·J

DETAIL·M

SECTION·G-G

DETAIL·C

SECTION·A-A

SECTION·K·K

SECTION·E·E

DETAIL·N

DETAIL·F

DETAIL·L

SECTION·D·D

DEAN KENNEDY·1932

▿ MANTEL ~ THE · FISHER · HOUSE ▿
OLEY ~ BERKS · COUNTY · PENNA.

Doorway Detail

THE KNABB HOUSE, NEAR LIME KILN, PENNSYLVANIA

Doorway Detail
THE SPANG HOUSE, SPANGSVILLE, PENNSYLVANIA

DETAIL OF ENTRANCE

THE BARTON HOUSE,
CROYDON, NEW HAMPSHIRE

Early New Hampshire Homes

N ARCHITECTURAL pilgrimage through New Hampshire reveals the fact that the early settlers did not follow any fixed style in building their houses. There are no character-istics of mass or detail which occur often enough to make it possible to define a "typical" New Hampshire dwelling.

Portsmouth (Strawberry Bank—1623) and Hampton, the seaport towns, among the first to be settled, attracted a different type of settlers from those colonists who settled the inland towns of Exeter (founded in 1638 by the Reverend John Wheelwright) and Dover (founded by Edward Hilton, sent over from England about 1627), while the farmers sought their fortunes in the fertile valley of the Connecticut. The territory included in the Province of New Hampshire, which from 1638 to 1678 was within the boundaries of Massachusetts, was so large and so sparsely settled that there was small chance for the pioneers to adopt the building traditions of their neighbors. They were little disposed to union among themselves. They came from the other colonies bringing their local architectural traditions with them, and developed these to suit their new environment, producing results which are a constant surprise to the student of early American architecture as he wends his way about the State.

Owing to the many varieties of religious opinion that prevailed among the radical pioneers, each new group-ing and consequent settlement had an individuality all its own, determined by the personality of its leader and the ideas that he represented. The traveller should be prepared to find, therefore, even in the most unexpected places, many examples of early dwellings each with marked individuality. Take, for instance, New Ipswich, settled about 1735, a hamlet uncontaminated by the summer tourist, drowsing its way through the course of time in a beautiful setting of green hills and fertile val-leys. Here one finds the Laura Hooper House, simple, well proportioned, a farmhouse of the better type, and, near by, the imposing Barrett mansion with stables, outbuildings and all the appurtenances of a Colonial "Estate."

The General Reed House, at Fitzwilliam, is a fine example of the well studied composition of the later 18th-century period. The nicely proportioned doorway, perfect in detail, the well thought out fenestration and the accent of stability added by the quoins make the ensemble worthy of serious consideration by the mod-ern architect. This house seems to me to be as excel-lent an example of the "Colonial" as any I have ever seen. Out of the infinite variety of types and styles that make up our early architectural period, this house and a few others similar to it, scattered through the New England section, express the true conception of our pre-Revolutionary builders.

Houses like this one were developed to fit American conditions, life and manners at a time when people had leisure to study how to express the ideals of the Ameri-can family and hearth in the household arts. The early

American styles not only express our ideals, but, as a practical matter, are easy ones in which to design. Their forms are simple, suited to present-day methods of construction in contrast with the forms of other styles which are less direct and therefore more costly. They are certainly more appropriate than the pseudo-Spanish and Italian, the lath and plaster "half timber" and other "adoptions" that supply the present-day Realtor with his stock of "stage-scenery" masquerading as architecture.

The small farmhouse at Westmoreland is an interesting example of the beauty of simplicity. A foursquare, ridge-roof house has been made a lovely piece of architecture by good proportion, fine fenestration and an elaborately moulded doorway, with just a suggestion of rugged ornament that suits so well its background of simple clapboards.

This little town of Westmoreland, by the way, has one of the most beautiful situations in New England. Anyone whose patriotic pride has been dampened by a worship of the lovely, rural, English countryside should take the trip to this hamlet, ascend Park Hill and gaze

THE LAURA HOOPER HOUSE, NEW IPSWICH, NEW HAMPSHIRE

THE GOODENOUGH HOUSE, CROYDON, NEW HAMPSHIRE

ENTRANCE
DOORWAY
DETAIL

out upon the Connecticut Valley from that eminence. A more perfect picture of rolling hills, winding rivers and all that goes to make up an ideal landscape is seldom found. Were this spot near one of the "tourist centers" of Europe, it would be famed throughout the world. As it is, it is seen by perhaps a half dozen people a year, without counting the local inhabitants who are few and far between.

The Moulton House is a particularly interesting example architecturally, both within and without. Till a year or so ago it was at the crossroads in Hampton, a pathetic structure, slowly disintegrating. It was threatened at any moment with demolition, was then bought by Mr. Harlan G. Little, moved to its present setting and restored most sympathetically.

produced some detail that is original and full of naïveté. The little sub frieze of ornament in the location that is filled by dentils in the usual examples is a startling innovation that justifies itself by the finished results. The planning of a motive above the entrance of almost the same scale and design as the entrance itself is unusual to say the least. But is it not interesting?

Map of the Province of New Hampshire
Made in 1777—Showing the most inhabited parts

These artisans of our early days violated the very rules that present-day teachings pronounce necessary to good design for any artistic medium of expression. The inherent good judgment, culture, call it what you will, of some of our early builders was founded on taste and an appreciation of proportion that are very difficult to account for when there was no opportunity for architectural education as judged by modern standards. Can the modern farmer-carpenters produce the results that these pioneers obtained? For answer look about you in any "modern" American town. It is written indelibly in the jig-sawed ornaments, the "gothic" windows and other atrocities that fifty years of Victorian ugliness have left behind.

The rear has a most interesting gambrel wing, seemingly of a much earlier period than the main house. It was probably the first structure to which the main house was added.

The two houses at Croydon stand in a village of about five houses, and by their juxtaposition accentuate their absolute dissimilarity. The one with the fence and the arched doorway has a certain charm in being based on precedent, the beautiful cornice of the doorway having a more or less classic feeling of design. The Barton House next door is no less charming, but the designer here allowed himself free play and has

The period immediately following the War of 1812, except for isolated instances, saw the end of a style of architecture that has never been revived. Although we are on the verge of a renaissance now, the modern architect is just beginning to understand the true motives and subtle characteristics that underlie the work of

DETAIL OF ENTRANCE

THE GENERAL REED HOUSE,
FITZWILLIAM, NEW HAMPSHIRE

PARLOR—THE DEXTER HOUSE, CLAREMONT, NEW HAMPSHIRE

their predecessors, and the "Colonial" absurdities of the past decades are giving way to buildings designed by men who through study and knowledge have sensed the beauties of the old work and are incorporating them into their daily practice.

The interior of the house at Claremont and the china closet in the Bellows House at Walpole—while entirely different in feeling and execution—are both fine examples of the work of their periods. That in Claremont shows a sophistication and a delicacy that are almost Adamesque, while the Bellows china closet, of an earlier period, has an ingenious combination of moldings, etc., that perhaps will not bear minute analysis, yet in effect the whole is good.

The Swift House of Orford is entirely different from any of the other examples illustrated. It was probably built during the period which began about 1825, as it has many features that are not in keeping with the earlier work. The tremendous arched window in the pediment is out of scale, yet the general proportions of the façade are good and the brickwork has a lovely texture. The columnar entrances, of which this house has no less than three, are well proportioned and show a lively variation of detail. The wrought-iron railing over the front entrance porch adds the finishing touch.

FARMHOUSE NEAR WESTMORELAND,
NEW HAMPSHIRE

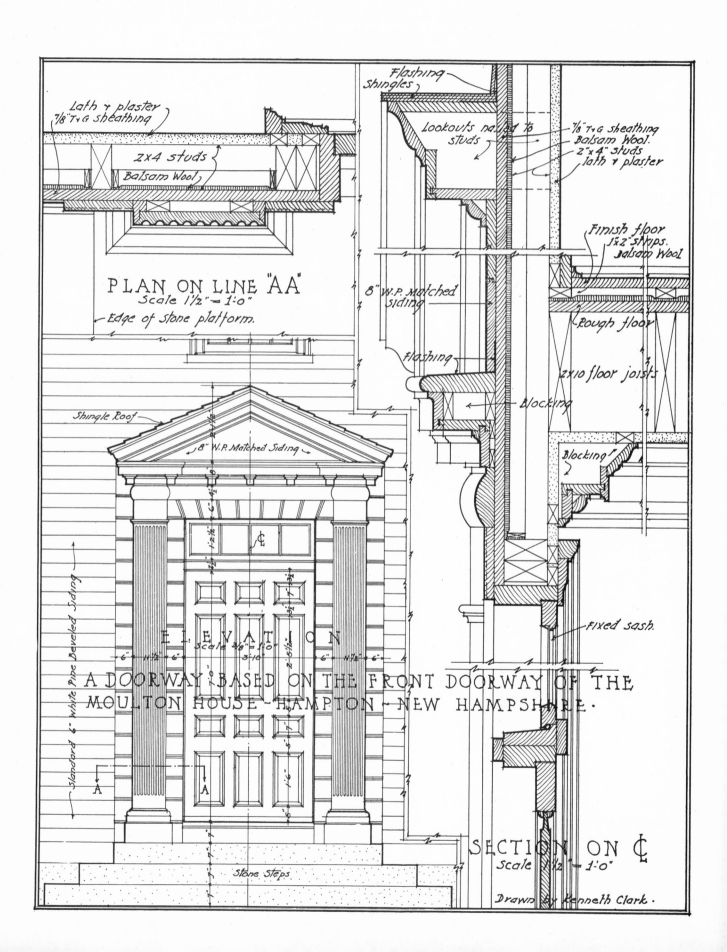

Lath + plaster
7/8" T+G sheathing

2 x 4 studs

Balsam Wool.

PLAN ON LINE "AA"
Scale 1½" = 1'·0"

Edge of stone platform.

Flashing
Shingles

Lookouts nailed to
studs

7/8" T+G sheathing
Balsam Wool.
2" x 4" studs
lath + plaster

Finish floor
1 x 2" strips.
Balsam Wool

8" W.P. Matched
siding

Rough floor

Flashing

2 x 10 floor joists

Blocking

Blocking

Shingle Roof

8" W.P. Matched Siding

ELEVATION
Scale 3/8" = 1'·0"

fixed sash.

A DOORWAY BASED ON THE FRONT DOORWAY OF THE
MOULTON HOUSE · HAMPTON · NEW HAMPSHIRE.

SECTION ON ₵
Scale 1½" = 1'·0"

Drawn by Kenneth Clark.

Stone Steps

Standard 6" White Pine Beveled Siding

A   A

THE GENERAL MOULTON HOUSE,
HAMPTON, NEW HAMPSHIRE

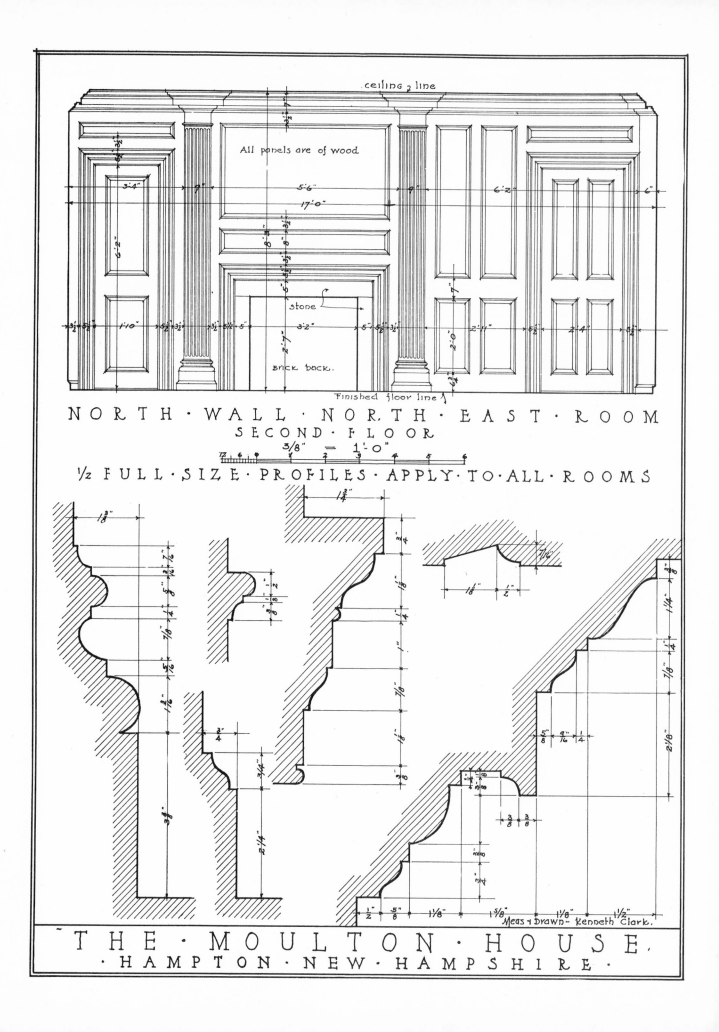

ceiling line

All panels are of wood.

stone

Brick back.

Finished floor line

NORTH · WALL · NORTH · EAST · ROOM
SECOND · FLOOR

3/8" = 1'-0"

½ FULL · SIZE · PROFILES · APPLY · TO · ALL · ROOMS

Meas & Drawn- Kenneth Clark.

THE · MOULTON · HOUSE.
· HAMPTON · NEW · HAMPSHIRE ·

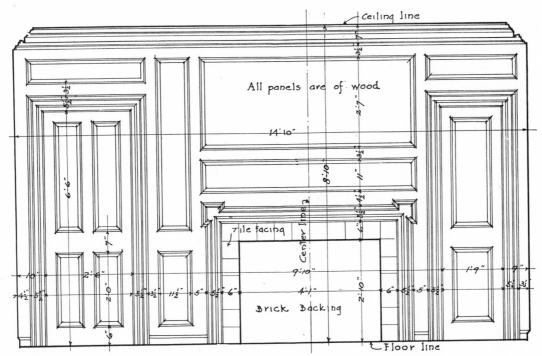

. N O R T H · W A L L · S O U T H · E A S T · R O O M
· F I R S T · F L O O R ·

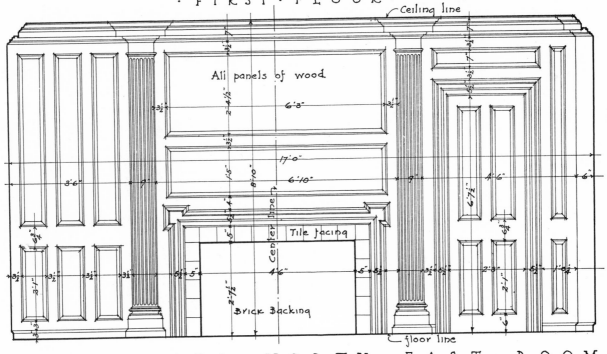

N O R T H · W A L L · N O R T H · E A S T · R O O M
· F I R S T · F L O O R ·

SCALE 3/8" = 1'-0"

Meas + Drawn Kenneth Clark.

T H E · M O U L T O N · H O U S E
· H A M P T O N · N E W · H A M P S H I R E ·

THE SWIFT HOUSE,
ORFORD, NEW HAMPSHIRE

DETAIL OF SIDE DOORWAY

62

The JOHN BELLOWS HOUSE
WALPOLE, NEW HAMPSHIRE

MEASURED DRAWINGS from
The George F. Lindsay Collection

THE CHINA CLOSET

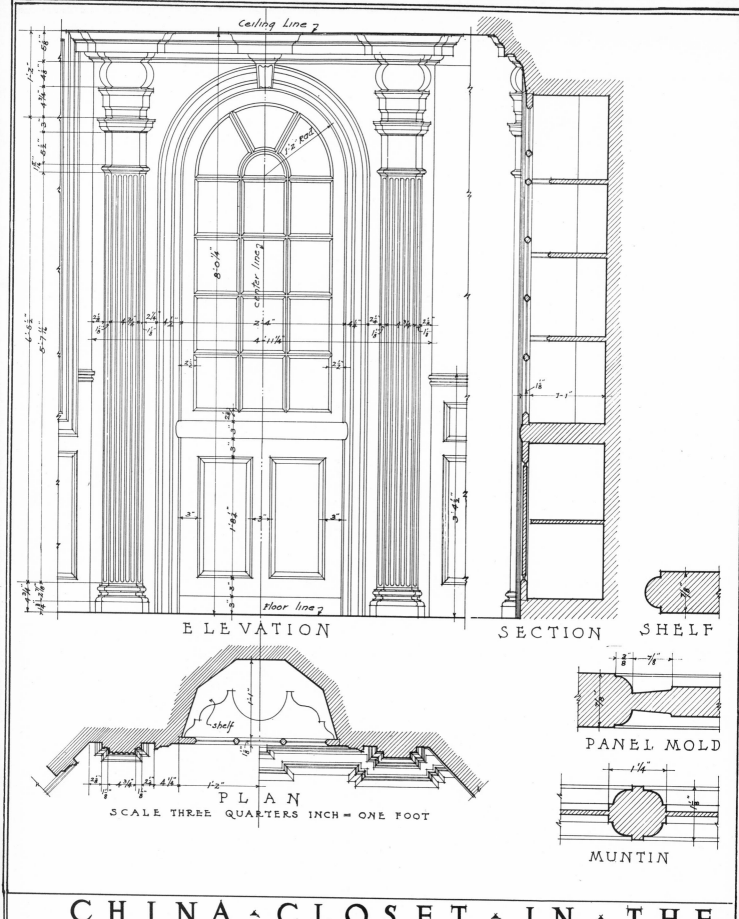

Ceiling Line

1'-2"
5⅝"
4⅝"
4¾"
3"
5½"

6'-5½"
5'-7½"

1'-2" Rad.

center line

8'-0¼"

2½" 4¾" 2¼" 4½"
⅛" ⅛"
2'-4"
4'-11¼"

2½"

2½"

4½" 2¼" 4½" 2½"
⅛" ⅛"

3½"

3"-3"-3"

3"
1'-8½"
3"
3"

3'-4½"

4¾"
⅞" 2⅞"

floor line

ELEVATION   SECTION   SHELF

shelf

2⅞" 4¾" 2¼" 4¼"
⅛" ⅛"
1'-2"

1'-1"

⅞"

PLAN
SCALE THREE QUARTERS INCH = ONE FOOT

1'-1"

⅛"

⅜" ⅞"

⅞"

PANEL MOLD

1¼"

MUNTIN

CHINA · CLOSET · IN · THE
· WALPOLE · NEW

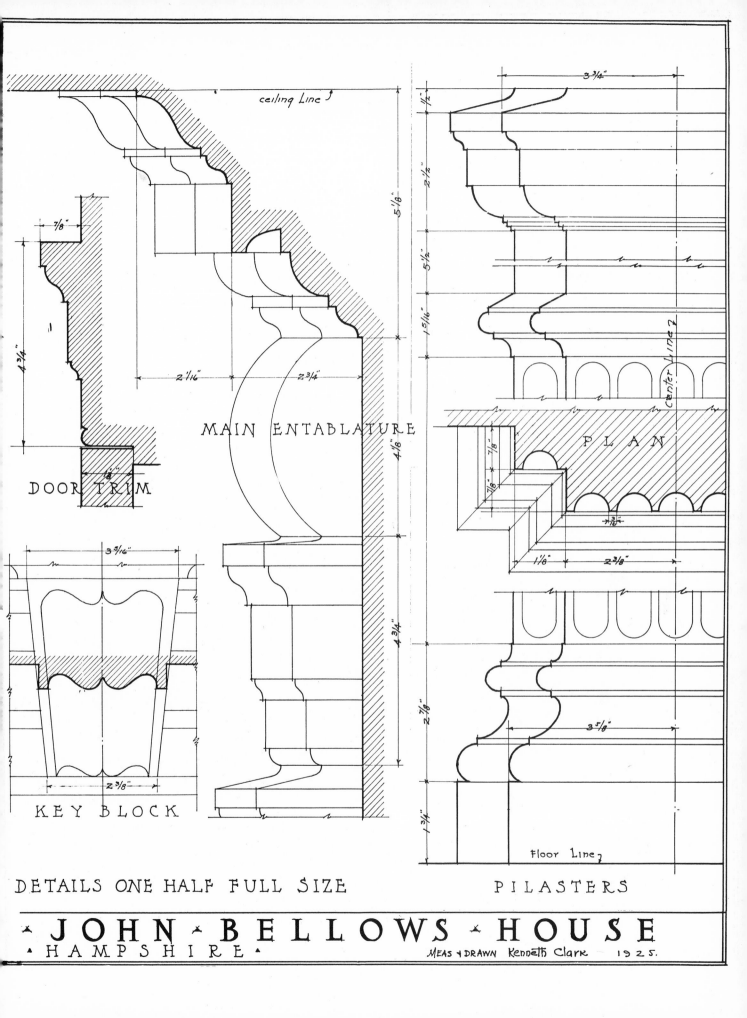

ceiling Line

MAIN ENTABLATURE

DOOR TRIM

KEY BLOCK

PLAN

PILASTERS

Floor Line

DETAILS ONE HALF FULL SIZE

JOHN · BELLOWS · HOUSE
· H A M P S H I R E ·

MEAS & DRAWN Kenneth Clark 1925.

STAIR HALL—THE VERNON HOUSE, NEWPORT, RHODE ISLAND
Built in 1758

SCALE·FOR·DETAILS·
1½" = 1'-0"

BALUSTERS ⅝x1"

GENERAL · PLAN
SCALE ⅛ = 1'-0"

NEWEL AT RAIL

2½

DETAIL · P
OF · NEWEL

2ND FLOOR   DOWN 20

FIRST FLOOR   UP 20

3'-9½

3'-9½   1'-0"

3'-9½

TION · OF · NEWEL · ETC ·

FLOOR LINE

1"X2" STRIPS

HANDRAIL MORTISE
FOR BALUSTERS

⅜ X 1 FILLER BETWEEN BALS

New England Woodwork

N WRITING of our early interior woodwork, or in illustrating it, one feels a
sense of restriction and a temptation
to wander from the chosen topic into
a treatment of old rooms as a whole.
Obviously a room is not complete
from an artistic point of view until it is furnished appropriately; old woodwork was but a part of that total
effect. That there was a marked relationship, particularly in New England, between the character of architectural detail and the furnishings of the several stylis-
tic phases is a fact needing wider recognition, since there
is always the easy path of unrelated mixtures.

Nearly all our old rooms have suffered such losses,
or accumulations, that both research and imagination
are required to gather together once more their scattered elements, the effect of charm and decorative entity.
Photographs and drawings serve as an introduction to
old interiors but, it seems, one must actually enter a
room to sense its scale, its proportions and the relation
of one part to another.

Our earliest interiors, those of the 17th century, re-
present a folk-art, medieval in character. By the begin-

ning of the 18th century a new style was evolved and,
due to the availability and use of builder's handbooks,
a sense of style was recognized from Maine to South
Carolina. Although we know changes in the handling
of this style varied according to time and place, yet
changes came slowly and young men were trained to do
and to think in the ways that would be expected of
them in their maturity. Every joiner, cabinet-maker,
housewright, carpenter, or carpenter-builder of the
18th century worked in the style of the time freely interpreted. All moulded work from the cornice of a high
chest to the cornice of a mansion was cut by hand with
planes formed to make the curved elements of this simple architecture of classical origin. There were quarter-
round, half-round, ogee, scotia, cyma forms, etc., in
planes of graduated sizes and these formed the key-
board upon which the designer or master workman
played his endless variations.

In the woodwork of both the 17th and the 18th centuries the element of craftsmanship is important. The
work of intelligent men, proud of a manual skill passed
on from master to apprentice or from father to son,
produced an ever fresh handling of well-known forms

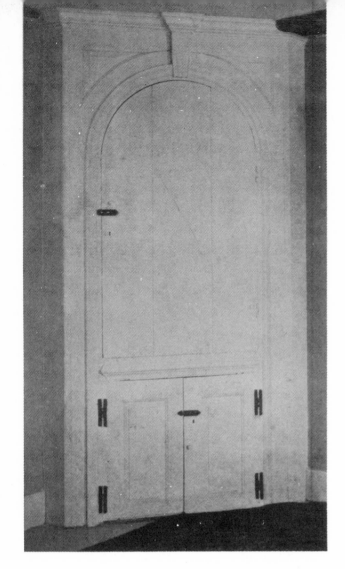

that were acceptable to several generations.

The architect of the present day may easily have a passing thought of envy in considering the directness, the co-ordination of artistic ways and means, that existed here in the 18th century. A scheme of interior woodwork had to be but sketched in a rough way, by the man who knew what he was about, and there were trained workmen all ready at hand with an established method and an ability to translate general ideas into finished work. To be sure they used and understood a

CORNER CUPBOARD

THE MORRIS HOUSE,
MORRIS COVE, CONNECTICUT

INTERIOR—THE OLD SHIP TAVERN, ESSEX, CONNECTICUT
Built by Uriah Hayden, circa 1675

INTERIOR—THE THOMAS LEE HOUSE, EAST LYME, CONNECTICUT

Original part of house built circa 1660

limited architectural expression but, according to their needs, they mastered it and that, perhaps, is why we respect an inheritance of their work which makes up in genuineness what it may lack in "impressiveness" or costliness.

For our purpose, four general divisions in this early woodwork may be made: The work of the 17th century and three phases of the 18th century; early, middle and late. The woodwork of the 17th century and that of the 18th sprang from separate architectural traditions; the earlier work had a kinship with the smaller provincial buildings, still Gothic in origin, of 16th century England. Our woodwork soon after the year 1700 was wrought in the Anglo-classic style but in New England it bore the stamp of a certain American independence.

Eighteenth century woodwork was truly "finish" in the present-day sense of the word; it was a lining whereas the work of the 17th century was structural, an integral part of the building. Interiors of the 17th century displayed their corner-posts, girts, summer-beams and

INTERIOR—THE NOAH WEBSTER HOUSE, WEST HARTFORD, CONNECTICUT *Built circa* 1676

rafters with a frank acceptance of the structure. This exposed framing, mostly of oak, with its sound joinery is peculiarly attractive in our less robust and economical times. As a general rule, sheathing was placed against interior partitions in random widths of white pine and moulded bands were cut on each edge. These "shadow moulds," aside from their decorative value to the room, helped to enrich the line where the boards met in halved joints. There are also instances of the use of such sheathing applied horizontally.

Doors were of the batten type, often of two vertical boards moulded at the joint, with cross battens near the top and bottom and such doors with their wrought iron hinges, latches and faceted nail heads have a simple attractiveness and charm. In fact rooms of this early period with their mellowed tones of grayish-brown, their straight-forward use of material simply adorned, their sturdy joinery and huge fire-places have a rough honesty and strength which appeal to us, at times, as

do old ships framed of oak and with an appearance of readiness for all weather—fair or foul.

For our second division there are the rooms of the earlier part of the 18th century in the new style with chimney breasts, dadoes, and even whole walls paneled with a breadth and simplicity in keeping with a general sense of design seen also in the furniture and silver of the time. Although walls were sometimes enriched with a pilaster treatment, the detail in both pilasters and cornices has a certain restraint and quietness that differentiates it from similar work of the mid-18th century. This is well indicated in a room in the Webb house at Wethersfield, Conn.

A general lack of mantel shelves is characteristic of these earlier rooms; bolection mouldings framed the fire-place openings and were also used to frame doorways and the wall panels. Doorheads were often semi-circular in form and shell-top cupboards belong especially to this period. It seems necessary to add that

CORNER CUPBOARD
THE WEBB HOUSE,
WETHERSFIELD, CONNECTICUT

"WASHINGTON CHAMBER," THE WEBB HOUSE, WETHERSFIELD, CONNECTICUT

THE WEBB HOUSE "HOSPITALITY HALL" WETHERSFIELD, CONNECTICUT

Built for Joseph Webb, circa 1753

MAIN ENTRANCE DETAIL

DINING ROOM, THE WEBB HOUSE, WETHERSFIELD, CONNECTICUT   *Built circa 1753*

STAIR HALL—THE WEBB HOUSE, WETHERSFIELD, CONNECTICUT

Built for Joseph Webb, circa 1753

NORTH EAST ROOM—FIRST FLOOR (PARLOR) THE WEBB HOUSE, WETHERSFIELD, CONNECTICUT
Built, circa 1753

against comparatively simple woodwork, decorative richness was gained in the occasional use of the popular "japanned furniture," and the general use of colorful needlework and other textiles.

In New England during the mid-18th century there is evidence of a richer and bolder treatment of interior detail in keeping with the vigorous handling of furniture design then indebted to the school of Chippendale. There was a more elaborate treatment of the chimney breast, now generally fitted with a mantel, and a use of carving, consoles, "eared" architraves, fuller and richer cornices and pediments both plain and broken. One thinks of carved furniture with claw and ball feet, varied and elaborate chair backs, sofas of generous proportions and looking-glass frames with scroll and broken pediment forms as representing the spirit of this period. This same vigor in form and decoration

applies to the work of the silversmiths.

The mansion-houses of Maryland and Virginia had greater variety in interior woodwork at an earlier date than did the fine houses of New England.

The change in general taste is well seen in two important houses at Portsmouth, N. H., the Warner House (1728) and the Wentworth-Gardner House (circa 1760). The drawing-room of the Warner House, for example, has large bolection mouldings surrounding the fire-place, and around the arched door frames, smaller bolection mouldings surround the raised panels. The cornice of few and stout members is without dentils or modillions—there is a bold simplicity. A similar room in the Wentworth-Gardner House of about 1760, has a fuller treatment of the cornice, one room has a full entablature, and the stair hall with much enrichment and variety of elements, has both a dentil course and modillions in its cornice. Doors are rectangular; the architraves are flattened and also "eared" in several rooms.

However, although we may form our impressions of the works of a time upon dated examples there is a reservation to be kept in mind. In towns remote from the great centers they were slow to change and old tradition held on and a house with all the appearances of having been built about 1730 in the vicinity of Boston or Newport may be as late as 1750 in the valley of the Connecticut River.

The interior woodwork of the last quarter of the 18th century and of the early years of the 19th had attained a refinement, and at times an attenuation, which differed in the extreme from all earlier work. This was the time of subtlety and sophistication in design and not only planning but the attempt to visualize a result on paper became the aim of the planner of these later houses. Many fine houses of an earlier time had been outlined in a casual way by the owner and with general instructions for the parts such as "to be finished like Curnall Smith's loer rume." Much was left to the eye of the builder. In these later rooms, however, details and proportions were carefully studied in a drawing-board manner.

Such woodwork formed the natural background for refined furniture in the style of Heppelwhite or Sheraton, for delicate mirror frames, fine porcelain and silver with elegance and grace both in its form and its engraving.

Moulding forms had changed from the profiles adapted from the simpler orders to quirk-moulds of fine scale; there were delicate beading, elliptical sections and areas. An ornamental treatment was evolved by forming running patterns of gouge cuts and small borings usually in the frieze of a cornice. Toward the end of the century modelled reliefs in French putty were applied to mantelpieces, doorheads and cornices and this method of "putting on style" probably caused others before us to refer back to "the good old days." However, from the vantage point of an additional hundred years or more we see in this unassuming work of the 18th century three old essentials of good architecture, "a regard for Beauty, Necessity and Tradition."

INTERIOR—THE BURNHAM HOUSE, IPSWICH, MASSACHUSETTS
Built between 1638 and 1670

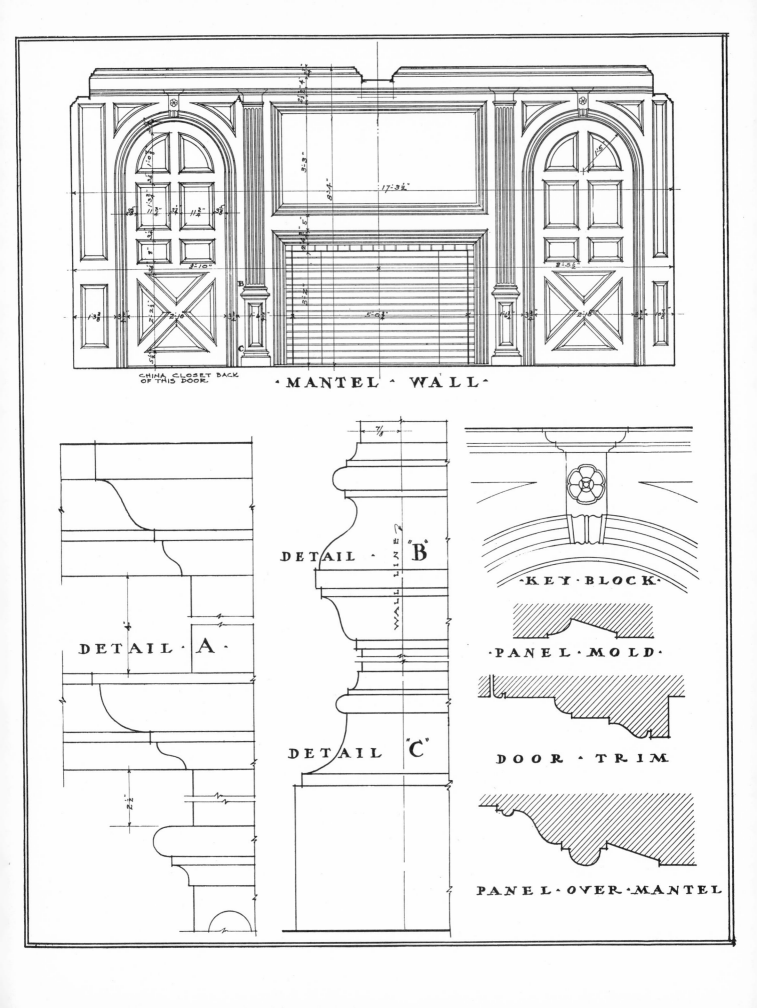

CHINA CLOSET BACK
OF THIS DOOR

· MANTEL · WALL ·

DETAIL · A ·

DETAIL · "B"

DETAIL "C"

· KEY · BLOCK ·

· PANEL · MOLD ·

DOOR · TRIM

PANEL · OVER · MANTEL

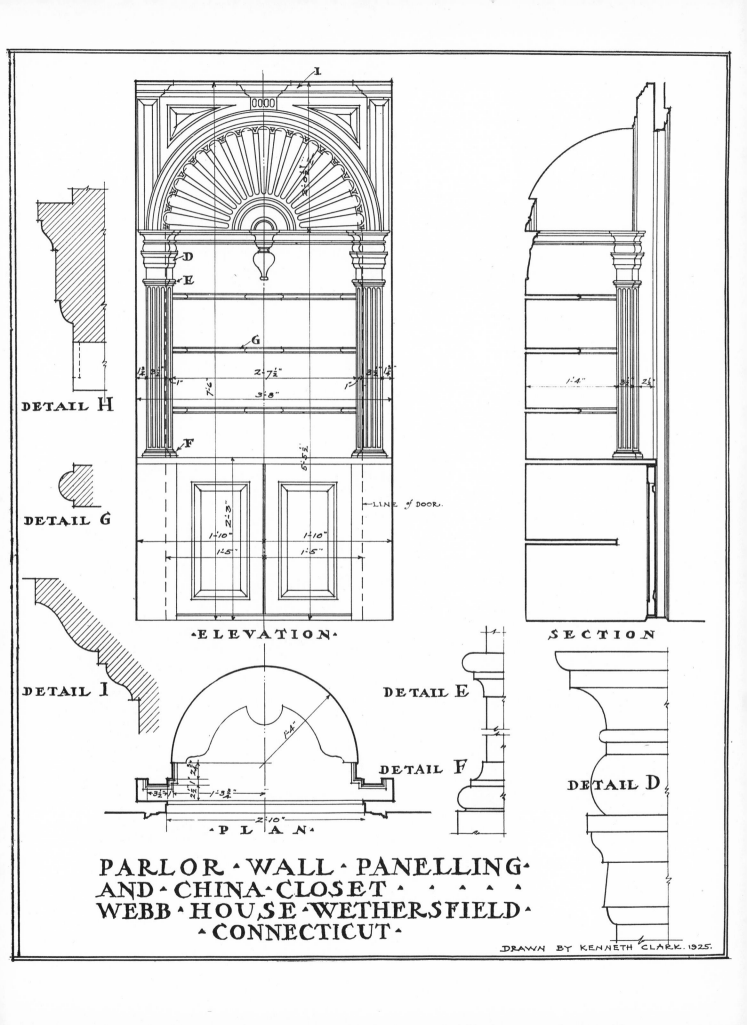

DETAIL H

DETAIL G

DETAIL I

·ELEVATION·

LINE OF DOOR.

SECTION

·PLAN·

DETAIL E

DETAIL F

DETAIL D

PARLOR · WALL · PANELLING ·
AND · CHINA · CLOSET · · · ·
WEBB · HOUSE · WETHERSFIELD ·
· CONNECTICUT ·

DRAWN BY KENNETH CLARK. 1925.

THE JENKS-GREENLEAF HOUSE. Detail of Doorway.

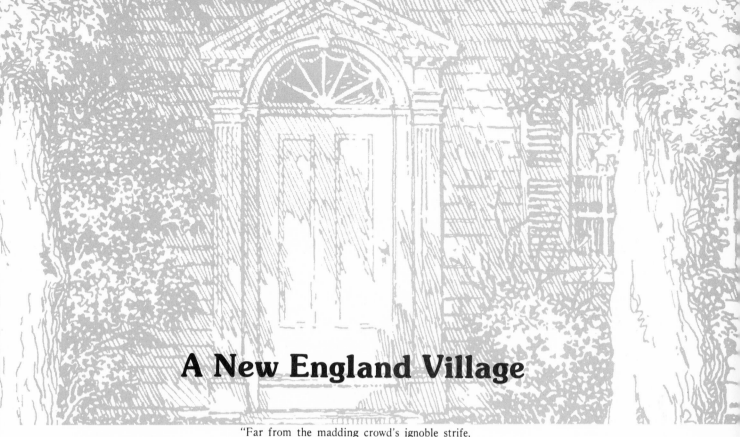

A New England Village

*"Far from the madding crowd's ignoble strife,
Their sober wishes never learned to stray;
Along the cool, sequestered vale of life
They kept the noiseless tenor of their way."*

WHEN Zabdiel Podbury fled from Stoke-on-Tritham in the Spring of 1689 with Drusilla Ives, taking passage on the bark *Promise,* sailing for Massachusetts Bay, it was not realized at the time that, from this union, and the joint labors of the Penthesilean pair, the village of Stotham (so named by them in memory of their autochthonous abode) would in later days come to be regarded as a typical example, although, perhaps, not so well known, of the unspoiled New England Village.

The terms typical and unspoiled are used advisedly, as a reference to the illustrations will show. There are, possibly, no especially striking or far-famed structures, no wealth of fine carving or ornamental detail, no grand estates or mansion houses, yet from its early simplicity, and quality of chaste primness, the village has slowly developed, until, as it now stands, a characteristic chapter of New England endeavor lies spread out on the gently undulating plain, lapped by the salt waters of the inland cove on one side, and stretching out by the fertile meadows of the river on the other. The first temporary houses soon gave way to more permanent structures, and the tradition of restrained, conservative building has been faithfully followed even to the present day.

Fortunately there was no occasion, and, what is more unusual, no inclination to depart from the customs and practices of the earlier settlers, in buildings of a later period, and the blighting hand of the real estate promoter, and the withering touch of the speculative builder, are conspicuously lacking.

To the Podbury family—who may well be termed the founders of Stotham—eleven children were born, seven boys and four girls. Adoniram, who married Hephzibah Jenks, died in his early thirties, and the descendants of his widow, who afterwards married Theron Greenleaf, still keep up the old Jenks-Greenleaf house, the doorway of which is shown in the frontispiece.

Ira Podbury married Serena Bellows, and their son Manasseh, afterwards a colonel in the Stotham Fusileers, who made an enviable record in the Revolutionary War (*q.v.* Bilks' "History of the Early Revolutionary Volunteer Guards Associations" and Cranitche's "Curious Antiquities of New England Villages," pp. 329–427 *et seq.*), the financier of the family, built the second Podbury-Ives house, which was the pride of the village.

Obadiah and Nahum Podbury died in their early youth, Elnathan was lost at sea, but the youngest son, Obijah, early developing a natural instinct and taste for building, constructed, with the assistance of three others of the first settlers, many of the simple old farm-houses, a few examples of which are illustrated in the following pages.

Of the four daughters, Keturah, Mehitabel, Evelina and Zoë, nothing is known, except of the youngest. Zoë married Heman Billings, and the Billings house, designed by Speat, a Scotch architect, with its sloping gardens, gently terracing down to the river, has been kept in almost per-

The only farm-house in Stotham concerning which the records show lack of authentic data.

fect condition, altered but slightly and with reverent care, as evidences of the relentless tooth of time began to show here and there, until even now its pristine charm is but rounded and enhanced, mellowed and softened, forming a part of a well-nigh perfect example of simple domesticity and dignified unity of fitness of structure to the enframing landscape.

Generations of blushing maidens have swung on the old Billings gate, opening on the path leading to the meadows, in the pale light of the harvest moon, lending shy ear to the rustic swains of the village, as in whispered and halting phrases they spoke of their hopes and aspirations; and as a result of these meetings, old traditions were kept alive, and more and more houses were built and hearthstones kept bright, sanded floors neatly traced in swerving lines, and the simple life of the early settlers passed on through the mellowing influences of time.

Cadwallader Simpkins came to Stotham in 1734 in company with Barzillai Plainfield and opened a general store. Ebenezer Rogers' tannery down on the salt marsh meadows was just starting at the time, and the firm of Simpkins and Plainfield, which had prospered since its inception, undertook to finance the tannery business, and started a shoe and harness shop in a small way as a side line. From the very beginning the venture prospered, and the tannery grew and the shop expanded into the old stone factory, with its easily obtainable water power from a natural dam, slightly enlarged and extended by building a mill race, running close by old Obed Stowe's place.

Ebenezer was astute enough to retain control of the business, while duly sensible of the help he was receiving from the proprietors of the general store, and in the course of time amassed a considerable sum of money for those days. He was a generous contributor to the Congregational church—not the one shown in our illustration, but an earlier type, on whose sturdy foundations of rubble the new church now stands. Barzillai Plainfield retired from business while still in the hale and hearty forties, and

The house which Obijah Podbury built for his stepbrother Nahum Bodkins.

built an almost palatial mansion, for its simple surroundings, yet the details are well contained and the ornament sparingly applied.

There is a curious story, too long to be related here (for complete details consult Cranitche's "Antiquities," Vol. XIX, from which sterling work many of the facts here related were drawn), concerning the Rogers mansion, better known under its local title, as the "Haunted House," or the "House of Buried Treasure." Briefly, its outline is as follows:

Ichabod Somes, a wild, untamed, red-headed youth of the village, ran away at the age of sixteen, and shipped before the mast on the privateer *Polly,* at the beginning of the French and Indian Wars. Ichabod appears to have been a strapping youth, tall, and well formed for his age and of callipygian aspect. In later years it used to be said by the few who were fortunate, or unfortunate, enough to have encountered him, that his single remaining eye, the other having been lost in one of his numerous encounters with Barbary pirates, possessed a

This house was entirely constructed of material cut on the spot.

peculiar basilisk quality before which even the stoutest heart quailed, and the most resolute spirit became as weak as babbling waters.

After many and various adventures, enduring through a period of some ten or a dozen years, during which time Ichabod had, by sheer force of dominance, attained command of a vessel of his own, all trace of him became lost.

Meanwhile the Rogers mansion suffered many vicissitudes. An old darkey servant, named Phinehas Moseley, was discovered one frosty December morning on the floor of the wood-shed, with his throat cut from ear to ear. It happened that the family were away at the time, and the crime would not have been discovered so shortly after its committal, had not Gershom Judkins, Obijah Podbury's foreman and right-hand man, happened to be passing by, and, as it was a cold morning, knowing that the Rogers family were away, decided to step in for the wicker demijohn of Santa Cruz rum that old Phinehas had drawn off from the Rogers rum barrel, a little at a time, so that the gradual

Old farm-house on Sandy Point, built by Obijah Podbury.

THE CADWALLADER SIMPKINS HOUSE.
The large shagbark in the front yard was planted at
the time of the raising of the frame of the house.

lowering of its contents would not be noted by the family. Appalled by the sight that met his eyes as he entered the wood-shed, he dashed out with a cry on his lips, only to be intercepted by a tall bearded stranger, with a single piercing eye, who neatly and deftly knocked him down with a staggering blow from the butt of his derringer.

These details were only learned little by little at a later period, for, when discovered, foreman Judkins was picked up for dead, and never completely recovered from the effects of the terrible blow.

The Rogers house was found to be intact, except for the loss of some valuable papers, in particular the deeds and description of the Rogers title to certain meadow lands, some overseas securities in the Dutch East India Company, and a considerable amount in pieces of eight, that were known to have been locked up behind a secret panel in the dining-room wainscoting.

Somes, who by now had acquired a very unsavory reputation, through reports that had trickled into Stotham from time to time, whether rightly or wrongly, was always popularly considered to have committed the crime (a tunnel leading from the wine cellar, where the rum barrel stood, to the outbuildings, furnished a ready means of access and escape to one familiar with the secret of the house and grounds, as Somes undoubtedly was), mainly from the fact that a large heavy derringer, marked with a skull and cross-bones, intertwined with the initials "I. S." (now under a glass and mahogany case in the rooms of the Stotham Historical Society in the basement of the Town Hall), was picked up in the back yard near the wood-shed.

Strangely enough, Rogers and his wife never returned to Stotham. All trace of them was lost, and the house was closed for years. After a time it came to be called the "Haunted House," and was shunned and avoided by all.

Later generations forgot the qualms and fears of their forebears, and, in spite of its atrabilarious appearance, became quite proud and boastful of its notoriety. Many strangers wandered out through the daggle of the front yard on sunny May afternoons, poking around here and there, first under the marble tiles of the piazza (which came over in ballast in the Peruvian bark

Calisaya from Demerara), and afterwards through the main rooms and closets, seeking whatever might be found of interest, in the hope of discovering some trace of the Rogers property, or some clew left by the assailants of Phinehas Moseley.

Thus the old Rogers house gradually disappeared, melting away slowly, baluster by baluster, and door by door, until the Historical Society finally claimed the poor scarred remains for its own, and, for the last thirteen years, has kept the vestiges of the departed grandeur and the boast of Stotham from the despoiling touch of the vandal.

A very beautiful and quaintly carved pine mantel from the Rogers front parlour has been set up in the room of the Society, together with a console from the dining-

DETAIL OF BALUSTRADE FROM PORTICO OF
THE ROGERS MANSION.
The original baluster, from which these were copied, is
said to have been brought from Baltimore.

room door frame, carved out of a solid white-pine plank, three and three-quarters inches thick and thirty inches long, portraying the birth of Ariadne. It was rescued in almost perfect condition, and still retains all its pristine freshness without a crack or flaw. The cornice of the porch, some of the columns, and a few of the balusters may also be seen.

In detail the balusters over the front porch show touches of Southern influence, and it is said they were copied from a pattern brought home by Ebenezer Rogers, who traveled often to Baltimore, where he had many business and social connections, while still active in the affairs of the tannery.

Main Street winds gently up-hill from the village square, lined with stately elms and locusts.

THE SALMON WHITE HOUSE ON MAIN STREET.
The clapboards were originally painted a deep saffron, but this has lately been
changed and the effectiveness of the house somewhat diminished in consequence.

THE SALMON WHITE HOUSE. Detail of Main Façade.

The spider-web window in the second story is from sketches by Robert Adam.

THE PODBURY-IVES HOUSE. Front Door Detail.   Ruben Duren, Architect.

Note that the wide necking of the pilasters is not at all inhar-
monious in combination with the frieze and architrave above.

THE PODBURY-IVES HOUSE. Ruben Duren, Architect.
Forms a chaste silhouette on the heights overlooking the river.

On each side are the principal residences of Stotham's prominent citizens. The Beriah Matthews house, now owned by two very charming maiden ladies, who still serve steaming, fragrant Bohea in fragile Chelsea, with crisp buttered Cassava biscuits fresh from a hot trivet in the east parlour, at four-thirty precisely each afternoon, is quite as interesting in its interior as the promise of its exterior indicates.

To one who has enjoyed the privilege of assisting on those occasions, it is a pleasure rarely to be experienced elsewhere, to hear and listen to their delightful conversation, to follow the reminiscences so quaintly worded, and to experience the gentle glow of their charming hospitality.

It is the personal contact with the people themselves that lends an elusive charm to the externals of their environment. As the houses seem to show by their aspect, they are the personification, in their external and internal attributes, of the simplicity of life, and the friendly point of view, of the gentle folk who live in them.

This is true of the Silas Mann house, now occupied by his great-grandchildren (Silas Mann

amassed a fortune in the East India trade, and the east dining room is still the most perfect example of Chinese Chippendale extant in New England). It is also true to a lesser degree of Gideon Pond's house and the slightly older Joab Hubbard house. Salmon White's house, sometimes called the Crocus house, on account of the peculiar shade of saffron originally used on the sidings, had a somewhat quaint origin: the main facts, of which the following is only the briefest abstract, were obtained from a pamphlet on the shelves of the Historical Society, entitled "A Short Account of the Experiences of Salmon White on the Sailing Vessel *Roxanne* from Stotham Narrows to Lucca, Anno Domini MDCCXCIX," published by Asher Harrison, 12½ Main Street, Stotham, June, 1823.

At the age of thirty-seven Salmon White, at that time just recovering from an attack of enteric anæmia, shipped as supercargo on the brigantine *Roxanne* in ballast for Lucca. After a passage of one hundred and nineteen days, during which head winds and cross currents were encountered, and many hair-breadth escapes from the dangers of the deep, all faithfully set forth in the log of Captain Eldad Bottomly, the island of Teneriffe was raised, four points sou'-sou'-west by west off the larboard bow, on the morning of October 23. Dropping anchor in the harbor of Risotto, at the base of the famous peak of Teneriffe, at that time possessing an unenviable notoriety as the haunt of buccaneers of the Spanish Main, it was learned that a young Scotchman by the name of Robert Adam was extremely anxious to leave the island at the earliest possible moment, as well he might be, having been marooned there when all, save he, went down in the wreck of the *Bouncing Betty*.

Young Adam and the supercargo soon struck up a warm friendship, due partly to a natural sympathy in ideals, and cemented permanently by the happy faculty which White possessed in the mixing of Santa Cruz sours, a beverage that young Adam declared topped his favorite negus by several pegs. After a few slugs of this delectable stingo had been brought to a perfect blend with the swizzle-stick, wielded by the deft fingers of a master of the craft, Adam, learning that White, on his return to Stotham, intended to erect a newer and more appropriate house for a man of his circumstances and constantly growing family, whiled away the long hours of the dog-watch by making rough sketches for his new friend, showing, in more or less detail, the inspiration that pervades the southeast façade of Salmon White's house, the peculiar arrangement of the staircase, and more especially the mouldings around the inside of the main door framing.

Some of these sketches may now be seen on the walls of the Historical Society, and a close scrutiny reveals the initials "R. A.," faintly traced in sanded ink, on the lower right-hand

THE HEMAN BILLINGS HOUSE.

side of some scraps of paper, evidently torn from the ship's log, on which they were made.

In particular, the spider-web window which adorns the main façade, shows the influence of Adam, though its execution lacks finesse, and may be said to have an original quaintness on that account, not always observed in the works of the famous brothers who afterwards became the vogue, and developed to a high degree of delicacy the more sturdy forms of their predecessors.

Space will not permit mention of all that is of interest in Stotham, fascinating as even the most

URIEL UNDERWOOD'S HOUSE FROM THE RIVER.
The proportion and balance between the outbuildings and the main house is particularly good.

casual study of its history may be, but some of the more prominent structures must not be allowed to pass without a note here and there, to call attention to certain of their characteristics.

Obadiah Witherspoon's house at the head of the village green, now owned by Miss Sophronia Winterbottom, a grandniece of Obadiah's, where she takes in a few paying guests for the summer months, is the proud possessor of a portico worthy of the most careful study.

The details of the Ionic capitals and the modulation of the entablature have all been most faithfully and studiously wrought with reverent care, the capitals being hewn by hand out of solid blocks of the finest white pine, and, protected by frequent applications of pure white lead and Calcutta oil, they are as perfect and fresh as the day they left Lemuel Short's shop down by the old dam.

The house of old Joab Drinkwater, who married Corinna Kane in his sixty-ninth year, Corinna being then a mere slip of a girl, dazzled by the worldly possessions of the redoubtable Major of the one-time Stotham Fusileers, shows a façade of great restraint and dignity and at the same time a purity of outline and sense of proportion rarely excelled by buildings of that date.

Uriel Underwood's house, a view of which is shown from the meadows leading to the river, has a nice balance and relation of outbuildings to main structures that is worthy of careful analysis.

Consciously or unconsciously, the earlier generations of New England settlers seemed to strike just the right note of proportion, harmony, fitness, and, what is more impressive, the distinctive character of their lives in the design of their buildings. Even a glance at the exterior of their houses and the most casual study of the planning and material from which they were built, leads to the inevitable conclusion that here, at least, exists an indigenous architecture wholly suited to its purposes.

Almost more than in any other village, this quality is to be noted in Stotham, where the quintessence of naturalness finds its ultimate expression.

THE FIRST MEETING HOUSE OF THE STOTHAM CONGREGATIONAL SOCIETY.
Built on the foundations of an earlier church. The detail of the entablature and the modulation of the pilasters are more refined than those of the first church.

Editor's Notes to "A New England Village," by Hubert G. Ripley

Having read the exciting story of Zabdiel Podbury, Cadwallader Simpkins and the "wild, untamed" Ichabod Somes, and with a newly developed appreciation for the "restrained, conservative" architecture of Stotham, a "typical and unspoiled village," the reader may well wish to do further research in the Stotham Historical Society archives or in one of the several other sources so thoughtfully mentioned in the preceding chapter. Unfortunately his efforts will be rewarded with little success, for alas, there is no Stotham Historical Society. Nor is there a pair of charming maiden ladies serving tea daily ("at precisely four-thirty" each afternoon) in the Beriah Matthews house.

The truth is that there is no Stotham. The entire story was created of whole cloth at least a Yankee yard wide. Its imaginative author, Frank Chouteau Brown, one of the finest architectural authors to contribute to these volumes, apparently decided that he and his associates were getting a little stuffy and a spoof was needed to bring them back to earth. With editor Russell Whitehead's concurrence, he created a fictional town, Stotham, and peopled it with a collection of 18th century characters that would do a novelist proud.

Thus, Captain Eldad Bottomly, (as well as his "Island of Teneriffe, four points sou' sou'-west off the larboard bow") serve only as a New England "in-joke." Ichabod Somes' one remaining eye didn't actually terrify anybody, and if generations of "blushing maidens" did actually swing on the gate of the Billings house, it must have been some other Billings house in some other town, although we'll warrant they swung for the same reasons as Frank Brown would have theorized.

In our table of contents you will find the author's name as "Hubert G. Ripley," and, believe it or not, Ripley was Frank Chouteau Brown, just having some innocent, Downeast fun, with himself and his fellow writers. We wonder how many among them were in on the joke, how many, if any, of the thousands of architects who received the monograph from which this chapter was adapted, ever detected anything wrong. We do know that of dozens of knowledgable people we have discussed this series of books with, none has ever tipped us off on the truth about Stotham.

Our thanks to Dan Lohnes of the Society For the Preservation of New England Antiquities for the true story, and for the following identifications of buildings pictured in this chapter:

Page	Listed As	Real Identity
80 (upper)	Unidentified	Unidentified
80 (lower)	Nahum Bodkins House	Unidentified
81 (upper)	Unidentified	Unidentified
81 (lower)	House on Sandy Point	Joseph Lynde House, Melrose, MA.
82	Cadwallader Simpkins House	Aspinwall House, Brookline, MA.
83 (upper)	Balustrade of Rogers House	Abraham Mitchell House, Chester, CT
83 (lower)	Salmon White House	Abraham Mitchell House, Chester, CT
84	Salmon White House	Abraham Mitchell House, Chester, CT
85	Podbury Ives House	House in Bedford, MA
86	Podbury Ives House	House in Bedford, MA
87 (upper)	Heman Billings House	Champion House, E. Haddam, CT.
87 (lower)	Uriel Underwood House	Wheeler House, Oxford, NH
88	First Meeting House of the Stotham Congregational Society	North Woodbury Congregational Church, Woodbury, CT

Detail of Front Elevation
COLLIN'S TAVERN, NAUGATUCK, CONNECTICUT

New England Inns

The American Colonies were settled so rapidly that one of the earliest evidences of the new order was the establishment of a string of inns and taverns reaching from Massachusetts Bay to the Carolinas. The seaports, of course, had to provide accommodation for the constant stream of new arrivals, until they could find homesteads and build the lovely old houses, churches, court rooms, and town offices, many of which, so well were they designed and constructed, are still cherished monuments of XVIIth and XVIIIth century culture. The Old State House in Boston and the old court room in Yorktown are splendid examples of the Georgian style, than which no finer exist any place.

The designations "Inn" and "Tavern" are used interchangeably, though in comparatively recent times "Tavern" has come to mean a place where food and drink were served to travelers, while "Inn" means that lodging also may be had. What fragrant memories cluster around the mention of "The Bell in Hand," and "The Old Elm," for example, "The White Horse Tavern" and "The Bunch of Grapes" in Kingston. It was in this latter hostelry that the great American cocktail, at first christened the cock's tail, was invented. Whether the original Bunch of Grapes is still standing, I scarcely know; probably it was destroyed when the British, under Sir Henry Clinton, burned the town in 1777. Anyhow the history of the cocktail (whether authentic or not is immaterial) is a poetic legend and so fraught with romance that the telling of it may not be out of place here. We are indebted to "The Bumper Book," New York, 1899, for the tale that runs as follows.

Squire Allen, bluff and hearty, face a deep *bois de rose* o'erspread with indoor tan, dispensed good cheer to all comers at the aforesaid Bunch of Grapes. None need leave the Tavern thirsty whether possessed of the medium of exchange or not, for mine host kept a blackboard behind the bar, on which the customer's score was chalked up when specie or barter lacked. Good ale and strong drink flowed freely, and the Squire's buxom daughter, Betty, assisted her father in caring for the wants of the guests. When the stage coach from Albany arrived and the driver pulled in his foam-flecked horses, it was a busy time for them both, and Betty, her apron strings fluttering in the fresh breezes, her rosy cheek "like a Catharine pear, the side the sun shone on," as Sir John Suckling puts it, skipped lightly from table to table under the old apple tree with pewters of ale, trays of glasses, bowls of loaf sugar and water from the Old Well Sweep. Her father followed, a wicker covered demijohn under one arm, a black bottle of Sour Mash in hand, and a merry greeting for all.

When Leftenant Titheridge, with his hardy recruits, tall gallant fellows recently returned from the Plains of Abraham, appeared one day, and drew up his squadron in the yard between the early American wagon sheds with their row of elliptical arches, and the great hay barn, Betty was at the Well Sweep.

THE RICE TAVERN, KITTERY, MAINE

COLLIN'S TAVERN, NAUGATUCK, CONNECTICUT

"Allow *me!*" were his words, and dismounting quickly he strode with rapid strides across the intervening space to the well, flinging his reins to Sargent Simpkins as he did so.

"What a lovely spot!" he added. "I think we'll stay here for a while and rest up a bit. You men look tired."

As he spoke these words, his muscular arms manipulated the well sweep and, despite Betty's protestation, he carried two full buckets of ice cold water into the kitchen with the ease and familiarity bred of active outdoor life combined with the grace of manner that betokened a gallant soldier not unfamiliar with the salons of the quality.

"Oh sir!" said Betty, dropping him a curtsy, "I thank you. You must be awful strong!" and she blushed prettily and looked down in modest confusion.

"*Du tout!*" replied the leftenant lightly, for he spoke French fluently, and was fond of displaying his knowledge. In the midst of the slight embarrassment caused by the unexpected meeting of two extremely attractive young people of opposite sex (such an embarrassment would be most unusual nowadays, it may be said) the Squire appeared.

His face was like a thundercloud, the cause of which was not long in appearing. It seemed that the Innkeeper was greatly addicted to the sport of cockfighting and inordinately proud of his prize cock Excalibar, whose valour and skill in the cock-pit were renowned throughout the countryside. The exploits of this lusty fowl had gained not only a redoubtable reputation for its owner as a trainer and sportsman, but had also resulted considerably to his pecuniary advantage. Many envied him the possession of such a paragon, and, indeed well they might for never before in three counties had been seen such noble courage, finer breed, and staying qualities than displayed by this young hero of many a cocking main. His age was three years and seven months and he tipped the scales at 4 lbs. 14 oz., a very knight among birds with a plumed tail worthy of Agamemnon's crest. For two days Excalibar had been missing, the Squire had hunted for him high and low throughout the neighborhood and among his corn cribs. Nowhere could a trace of him be discovered. The prince of birds had been stolen!

Leftenant Titheridge looked thoughtful as he recalled a half-forgotten incident of the hike down the river, but he said nothing. It was solemn and dismal cheer for the guests that night at the Bunch of Grapes. Shortly after daybreak the next morning the young officer rode away, bidding his men await his return. Everyone at the Tavern was disconsolate. Even Sargent Simpkins, a fine upstanding young man with a prepossessing face, and an eye for a pretty gell, scarce remarked the nimble figure of the Innkeeper's daughter as she busied herself with her household duties, sweeping the taproom, sanding the floor in graceful arabesques, plucking green corn, and tending the marigolds and johnny-jump-ups, for her garden was the delight of all visitors. Night drew on apace and no leftenant appeared. Again a gloomy and dismal meal while the candles guttered unsnuffed and the Squire smoked pipe after pipe, refusing all conversation.

As dawn, the rosy fingered, came peeping o'er the hills, Sargent Simpkins felt a touch on his shoulder.

"*Qui va la?*" he muttered sleepily, for he had picked up a smattering of French during the hardships of the Quebec campaign.

"*Je,*" whispered the voice of Leftenant Titheridge, for it was indeed none other. He held something indistinguishable in the half light. It was Excalibar unharmed and in all the glory of his plumage, brilliant as when the rays of the rising sun tip with iridescent glow the towering walls of the Fred F. French Building on Fifth Avenue, or the first view of the 1933 Chicago World's Fair startles the astonished visitor.

The sensitive ear of Squire Allen, a light sleeper, caught the whispered conversation in the adjoining room, and slipping quickly into his small clothes, he pushed open the door. Catching sight of his matchless bird, he uttered a great shout that aroused the entire household. Soon the room was filled with a joyous throng of guests, retainers and soldiers. Even Betty, with a green joseph thrown hastily over her night rail, peeped shyly in with admiring glances at the handsome young officer who, after searching far and wide, had returned triumphant with his quarry. Fully recovered from the spleen and black humor of the past three days, the overjoyed host called for the best breakfast the house afforded, while Betty slipped off hastily to put into execution an idea of her own. Let us quote an extract from the tale itself.

"Now whether it were from excitement or nervousness, or whether, perchance, mistress Daisy had before discovered the secret, and held it close for a great event, certain it is that she mixed sundry drops of bitters and wine of roots, with a dram of good Kentucky whisky, the whole poured over some generous bits of ice (not a little luxury in itself), and they all drank of the beverage "to the cock's tail"—for Jupiter had not lost a single feather. And then the gallant leftenant sware bravely that, in memory of the event, the delectable mixture he had drunk should be known as a cock's tail through all the army."

[Note. The author seems a bit confused. He calls the charming inventor "Betty" instead of Daisy,

THE RICE TAVERN, KITTERY, MAINE

Detail of Front Elevation
WAYSIDE INN—1686—SUDBURY, MASSACHUSETTS

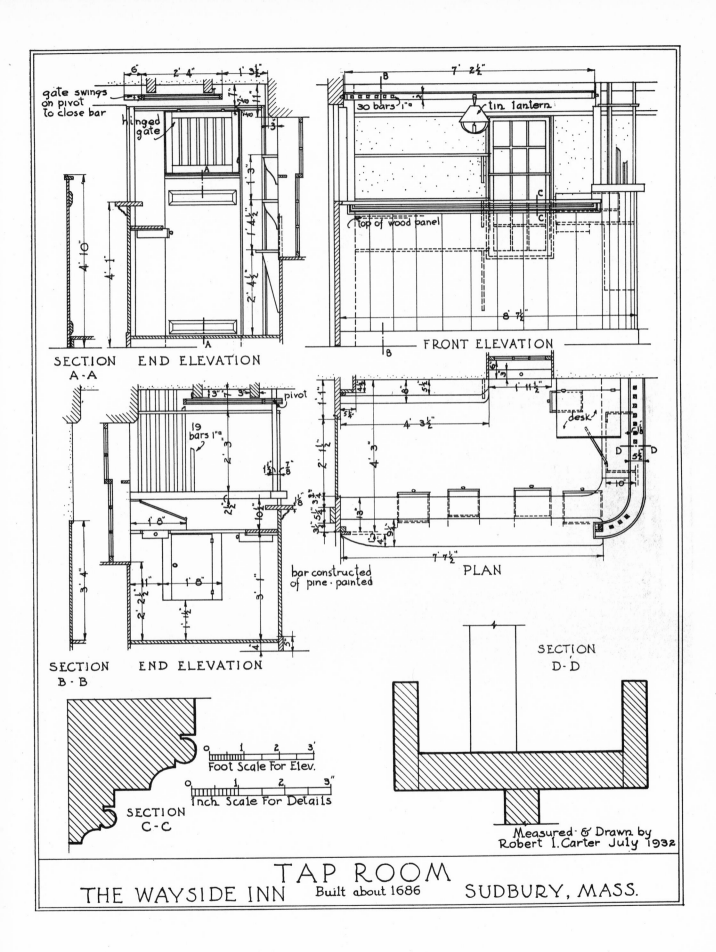

gate swings
on pivot
to close bar

hinged gate

SECTION A·A

END ELEVATION

30 bars 1"ø

tin lantern

Top of wood panel

FRONT ELEVATION

19 bars 1"ø

pivot

SECTION B·B

END ELEVATION

bar constructed of pine·painted

desk

PLAN

SECTION D·D

SECTION C·C

Foot Scale For Elev.

Inch Scale For Details

Measured & Drawn by
Robert I. Carter July 1932

TAP ROOM
THE WAYSIDE INN Built about 1686 SUDBURY, MASS.

TAP ROOM AND BAR—WAYSIDE INN—1686—SUDBURY, MASSACHUSETTS

and the gallant cock "Excalibar" instead of Jupiter. *Ed.* Well, maybe I did, memory plays us pranks at times, but what of it? *Author.*]

The subsequent adventures of Leftenant Titheridge and Betty [he means Daisy, *Ed.*] is not strictly concerned with the subject of New England Inns and Taverns and need not be dwelt on further. Interested students and Antiquarys will find more of it in the "Bumper Book," together with other timely knowledge.

One of our early recollections was a visit to the famous "Bell in Hand," located for over a hundred years in Pi Alley, Boston. This was strictly a Tavern and no other beverage, not even water, was served save good stout ale. Brie cheese, cold meats, coarse bread and hot mutton pies were available for the modest sum of five cents for each item. A "half with a dash," was the customary order, meaning a half mug of ale with a dash of porter. The ale was Bass', imported in barrels, and besides this a very special brand called Union Ale, which was smooth as silk and strong as the Hercules of Lysippus. About three full mugs of Union and you felt as if slammed by the Hero's club. The porter was bitter without being acrid, and seemed like velvet to the tongue. When drunken with brie cheese, its full flavor could best be appreciated. Customers almost always ordered half mugs (nothing but pewter was used in the tavern, by the way) in the belief that two halves were greater than a whole, yet so canny was the skill of the burly tapsters who drew the precious fluid, great husky lads with mighty arms, that it was a toss up either way. We've tried the experiment several times and never found that two halves caused an overflowing when poured together.

Many famous men were the inn's customers, and while the place was severely simple, Early American in character with wide pine boards and sanded floors, low ceilings and a few old prints on the walls, and while the clientele included almost every strata in our complex civilization from the highest to the lowly, I've never observed unseemly behavior or conduct that could be classed as an offense against good taste. When such men as Judge Palmer, the well-known authority on jurisprudence, Lieutenant Colonel Will, U.S.A., A.I.A., P.D., etc., etc., and Chelsea Joe, that polished devotee of the goddess of chance, patronize an estab-

lishment, one may safely follow in their footsteps.

Then there was "The Old Elm," a tavern that lent distinction and the aura of its personality to Tremont Street Mall in its declining years. This place was named from its proximity to the Washington Elm that grew opposite it on Boston Common. (The original Washington Elm was in Cambridge, of course, and the one on the common an offshoot from the parent stem.) Maybe there was once an "Old Elm" near the Cambridge tree, I don't know. Food was the main idea there, and the best *beer* in Boston, according to the local connoisseurs. We had our first glass of beer there when a student at Tech, and as I recall the incident, I was not greatly overjoyed by the experiment. It tasted strange and bitter. Since then, experience and wisdom have demonstrated the many excellent qualities of this ancient beverage when used with discretion. Weisse beer was also served there in babble glasses, great huge mugs holding a gallon, like the famous *"formidable,"* at the "Brasserie Lipp."

"The Old Wayside Inn" in Sudbury is perhaps the best known of all New England Taverns as the setting of the delightful tales of the lovable transcendentalist of the Golden Age. Though marred somewhat by the vandal hand of the great apostle of standardization and exploitation, it still retains much of its original charm when seen from certain view points, in spite of the absurdities of recent additions and strictures as to freedom of action imposed on its guests by the policy of its present owner. There are lovely old bedrooms, furnished right up to the last word of the present-day interior decorator's idea of just what an Early American bedroom should be, many pieces of really good old furniture, and the old bar and dining room practically as was, as far as anybody knows. There are glass cases containing General Witherspoon's sword belt worn at the battle of Bennington, some old pewter, a spinning wheel in the front hall that tangles up people's feet and warming pans and trivets and trammel irons (whatever they are) galore; quite a store of junk when all is told. The front porch is punk, but the clapboards on the walls, still painted the same old exquisite shade of salmon pink it has always worn, and the sweep of the hospitable gambrel, are still worth going miles to see.

THE WILSON TAVERN—1797—PETERBOROUGH, NEW HAMPSHIRE

OLD MILFORD TAVERN, MILFORD, NEW HAMPSHIRE

Entrance Porch
OLD MILFORD TAVERN, MILFORD, NEW HAMPSHIRE

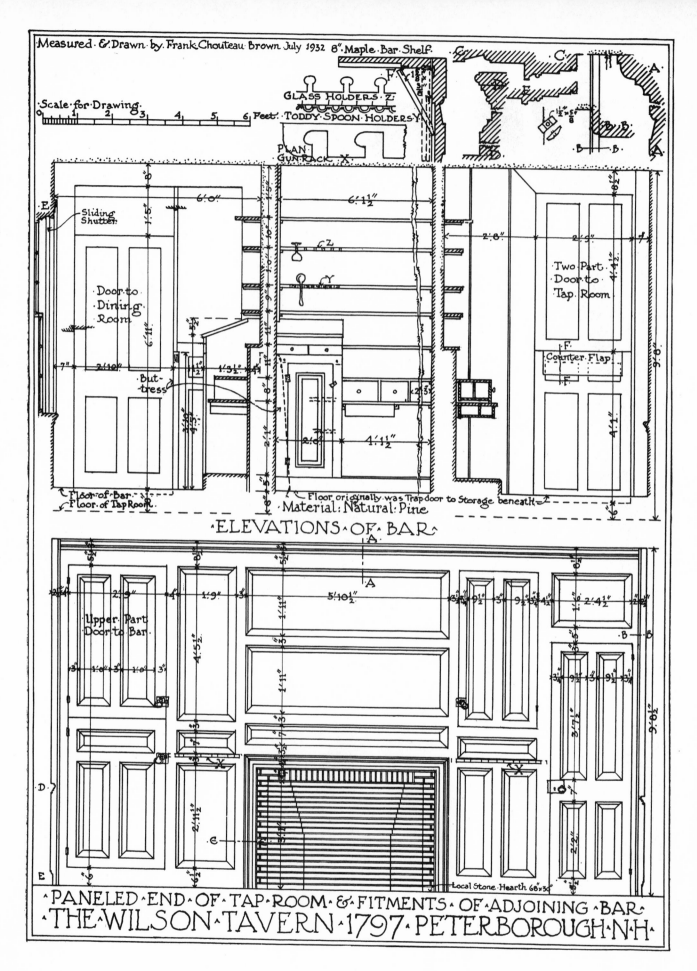

Measured & Drawn by Frank Chouteau Brown July 1932 · 8″ Maple Bar Shelf

GLASS HOLDERS · Z ·
TODDY · SPOON · HOLDERS · Y
PLAN · GUN RACK · X

Scale for Drawing

Sliding Shutter

Door to Dining Room

Buttress

Two Part Door to Tap Room

Counter Flap

Floor of Bar
Floor of Tap Room

Floor originally was Trap door to Storage beneath
Material · Natural · Pine

·ELEVATIONS·OF·BAR·

Upper Part Door to Bar

Local · Stone · Hearth · 66ˣ30

·PANELED·END·OF·TAP·ROOM·&·FITMENTS·OF·ADJOINING·BAR·
·THE·WILSON·TAVERN·1797·PETERBOROUGH·N·H·

102

TAP ROOM—THE WILSON TAVERN—1797—PETERBOROUGH, NEW HAMPSHIRE

TAVERN—1774—WEST TOWNSEND, MASSACHUSETTS

POST ROAD TAVERN, WESTMINSTER, CONNECTICUT

Early American Cornices, Part I

"CORNICE—*A large moulding which forms the coping of a facade or portion of a facade,—or surmounts a door, window, dresser, etc.*"—ADELINE'S ART DICTIONARY.

This is one definition of a cornice; it is *not necessarily* part of an entablature copied from Vignola.

THE early American house was in nine cases out of ten a square box-like structure of clapboards or plain shingles with a decorative doorway and an ornamental cornice as the sole relieving features of a design otherwise simple to the point of meagerness. On the remaining tenth of the houses, the most usual additional decoration was the superposition of small cornice-like heads to the windows, which tended only slightly to distinguish these houses from those with plain window trims; and the houses in which the whole facade was consciously "designed" constitute an incredibly small minority of the whole group.

Even within such narrow limits of design as were set for the colonial architects by their materials, the general poverty of the country, and the lack of training of the architects themselves, they managed to achieve a surprising variety in their houses, a variety evidently only capable of accomplishment by slight changes in the proportions of the masses of the buildings, and by the use of different decorative motives in the design of the two focal points of interest, the doorways and the cornices. That they were not without originality is amply proved by the amazing number of different solutions that they were able to discover, and this in spite of the fact that their design was *always* based on classic motives as interpreted by the Renaissance architects, and not (as at present) modified by knowledge of practically all historic styles. In part their freedom from the dominance of the dead hand of Vignola was certainly due to sheer ignorance; ignorance not so much of books, as of the fundamentals of architectural drawing which would enable them correctly to understand the illustrations, a fact which is amply proved by the many cases where the builder obviously tried to imitate drawings and failed in the same way that an ignorant contractor to-day fails to understand the meaning of detail sheets. Examine the cornice of the Post Road Tavern in which the general form of the Greek Doric order is approximately imitated, although no portion of it (and especially the triglyphs) is either clearly comprehended or correctly executed.

THE CAPTAIN ABRAHAM BURBANK HOUSE, SUFFIELD, CONNECTICUT
Built in 1736

Ignorance however, was but one and probably not the dominant factor in producing such free design; the Colonial architect was rather part of an architectural period than a copyist or interpreter of a past period, and was therefore totally unconscious of the need of consistency (if such need exists) which constantly hampers our modern designer; he never ran back to his collections of illustrations to see if others had done before him what he wanted to do; he probably had a certain amount of respect for precedent, but it was for precedent from which he could develop new motives, and not precedent as a storehouse containing all useful architectural motives.

The earliest form of cornice in America was really not classic at all, but derived from the English cottage, with which it was contemporaneous, and the plain treatment of the eaves (it can hardly be called a cornice) was continuously in use in very cheap work especially in the country districts, where either lack of funds or lack of technical skill in the carpenter made a built up, molded and decorated cornice impossible. This treatment persisted throughout colonial times, as is illustrated by the Hempstead house at New London, Connecticut

THE CAPEN HOUSE, TOPSFIELD, MASS.

THE HEMPSTEAD HOUSE, NEW LONDON, CONN.

and the Webb House at Orient, Long Island built more than one hundred and fifty years apart; and today in small, cheap work in the outlying districts we find precisely the same method of terminating a roof, used for the same reasons.

Aside from houses with these overhangs, practically every house built before, let us say 1790 had a cornice of strictly classic genesis of not much originality and in itself of little interest however excellent it may have been as a crowning motive. These cornices, (and detail in general) closely followed English motives, or rather English adaptations of classic motives, slightly decreased in scale as befitted the material, and as a rule pretty well proportioned to the masses of the buildings. Where mistakes in scale occur they are usually in the direction of overscale rather than the reverse, due perhaps to imperfect digestion of the English precedent, and failure to realize that the proportion of cornice to wall should be determined by the material and general scale of the surface as well as by height. From the earlier cornices we have little to learn which is not in Vignola; examine the Vernon house at Newport, Rhode Island built in 1758 and the Burbank house at Suffield, Conhecticut built in 1736 and it will be seen that we have in both cases typical classic cornices with consols, in one case with a dentil course below. There is no motive not ordinarily found in England at the same time, and while these whole cornices may be admirable crowning motives of the wall, they have no particular reason for illustration except as they explain the progress of the style.

by the use of pilasters against the wall, the frieze is entirely absent and the architrave suggested only over the pilasters with no corresponding breaks in the cornice or even the bed molds. The designer evidently had an idea which he did not quite know how to execute, but naïve as it is, it is nevertheless far more interesting than the correct cornices shown on pages 106 and 110.

THE WEBB HOUSE, ORIENT, LONG ISLAND

On the other hand the Shirley-Eustace house at Roxbury, Massachusetts built about 1750 has a very distinct character of its own. The corona is entirely absent, the soffit beginning under the bead at the bottom of the cymatium; practically all the bed moldings are decorated with combinations of historic motives as unexpected and curious as they are pleasing; and although an entablature would seem to be required

When we come to examine the cornices of houses built after 1790 we find that the genuinely classic cornice is as rare as it was common in earlier times. A simple succession of run moldings continued to make up the crowning motive of the plainer and cheaper houses, but on the larger and more ornate there was no limit to the play of fancy, or rather there was no limit within the means of execution by ordinary carpenters' tools.

It must be remembered in studying colonial work that there were no power planes—all run moldings were got out by hand—there were few capable wood carvers, and composition ornament for outside work was unknown. The tools with which the ornaments were executed were few and simple, but the extraordinary variety of designs which were executed, with gouges and molding

Now while the discussion of the sources of American design applies to all portions of the buildings, it is of especial force as regards the cornice, since as the use of cornices as methods of ornamentation became more and more extended, not only was the intersection of the roof and the wall treated with a cornice, but the doors, the window-heads, porches, rooms, mantels, mirrors

THE SHIRLEY-EUSTACE HOUSE, ROXBURY, MASSACHUSETTS

planes and especially with augers is amazing. Ornament sawn out with key-hole saws or turned on a lathe and applied to the surface of the boards is not infrequently found, especially in later work but ornament which could be done by a multiple molding plane and finished by a chisel or a gouge is by far the commonest, is perhaps the most ingenuously used, and is usually the best in scale with the light and graceful cornices of the period.

and even cupboards, were terminated by cornices of distinctly architectural character, and with little difference in the types employed. A cupboard cornice and the main cornice of a house differed in scale but not in character, and at the end of the century this was not the solemn dignity of classic design, but the free and playful translation of the cabinet-maker; the one difference being that in furniture vari-colored wood inlays

THE VERNON HOUSE, NEWPORT, RHODE ISLAND
Built in 1758

Detail of Cornice
THE BACON HOUSE, KENT, CONNECTICUT
Built in 1810

were often used to simulate flutes, wreathes or rosettes while the architectural ornament was always in relief.

The peculiar furniture-like cornice is as apparent in the books as in the executed work; and apparently the writers felt that no distinction was necessary between cornices used for various purposes, since page after page of cornices are

men technically not very skillful but with what was apparently a genuine feeling for detail, we find results which are elsewhere and at other times unequalled. Take for example the house at Chatham Center, New York built in 1798. This is not by any means the best designed cornice of the lot, and though not especially selected, will serve excellently to illustrate the

A HOUSE AT CHATHAM CENTER, NEW YORK

shown, the accompanying descriptive text giving no hint as to the portions of the building to which the authors thought them most appropriate; and in other pages where designs for mantels, doorways and houses are shown, the cornices are shown blocked out only, with the instruction that whatever cornice is most pleasing in the preceding pages may be used.

Drawn, as they were, from such sources, by

points above made. Its genesis is to be found in the Doric, but it has come a long way from its original. The pilaster on the corner has reeds instead of flutes; and the reeds have no proper termination, they merely butt in to the neck mold, which, by the way, most of us would consider not only a poor choice of molding but out of scale as well. The cap of the pilaster does not support the architrave but returns on itself against the frieze, and the molding which acts as architrave lines up with the bottom of the cap, yet does not intersect with it, and returns on itself as does the cap. Since the architrave is much smaller than the cap, the frieze is shorter at the corners than between the pilasters. The cornice itself is not far from certain classic examples, although the mutules are under-nourished, and the

amateurish piece of work, and yet one which shows a sensitive feeling for moldings, and a nice appreciation of the function of the cornice as a decorative band rather than a structural feature.

An entirely similar criticism can be made of the cornice of the Congregational Church at East Canaan, Connecticut The pilaster projects too far, and the entablature above shows no

A HOUSE AT EAST MARION, LONG ISLAND

guttae supposedly proper to the order are replaced by six round holes bored in the soffit in an ornamental pattern. The turning of the corner between the rake of the gable and the horizontal, always difficult, is here most awkwardly managed; really it is not managed at all. And what shall we say of the row of dentils like drops below the bed mold? Is this part of the cornice or a decoration to the frieze? Altogether it is a most

classic articulation; architrave, frieze and cornice are jumbled together so that it is practically impossible to describe portions of it as belonging to any one of the three. The corona is lacking, the fillet below the cymatium serves as corona, and the soffit is not countersunk; but the whole composition is a sound design for the crown motive of a rather important building.

The colonial designers seem to have been quite

THE CONGREGATIONAL CHURCH, EAST CANAAN, CONNECTICUT

THE GENERAL STRONG HOUSE, VERGENNES, VERMONT

strongly impressed with the value of recurring decorative motives as opposed to continuous decoration on the frieze, and we find very many cornices either with or without mutules, which have decorations on their friezes derived from the triglyph. In the example last referred to the principal ornament is a series of lozenge shaped pieces of wood counter-sunk in the frieze, and separated by sets of five upright reeds; this is certainly very reminiscent of the triglyph and

about 1820. Although it does appear somewhat out of place in a cornice of such mannered proportions as those of the Vergennes house. The contrast is especially bad between the series of black and whites of the row of consoles, the lesser row of dentils and the triglyphs. The triglyphs (which should be most important) are out of scale and insignificant by reason of their small size and lack of depth. In the "King Caesar" house at Duxbury, Mass., built in 1794,

"KING CAESAR" HOUSE, DUXBURY, MASSACHUSETTS
Built in 1794

metope, although the spacing of the ornament bears no relation to the spacing of the mutules. In the frieze of the house at East Marion, Long Island the triglyphs are represented by reeded pieces of board spaced on centers *between* the mutules; and these pseudo triglyphs do not extend the full height of the frieze to rest on the architrave, but are pendant from the bed mold. The treatment of the frieze of the house at Vergennes, Vermont is similar, but perhaps a little better done, as is natural in a house built

triglyphs are suggested by sets of three deep grooves cut in the lowest of the bed molds. This photograph shows another very characteristic and curious ornamental form which appears often in the cornices of the time: the rope ornament bed mold with auger holes bored in patterns, so that one hardly knows whether the designer intended to simulate leaves or rope. Perhaps he did not know himself, but at least he succeeded in producing a "color" of surface that is unique. The ornament is not altogether pleasant in such large quantities, as in the church at South Hadley, Massachusetts, where it is used not only as a principal bed mold, but also as the crown mold of the Doric cap, much as leaf ornament was used by the Italian architects of the Renaissance.

The same general type of ornament is used in the house at East Hartford, Connecticut but the placing of the auger holes has given this a distinctly leaf-like quality; and immediately below it we have a dentil course composed of guttae, which is not unusual at this period when the dentil course was a favorite motive and rarely used in its original form.

THE CHURCH AT SOUTH HADLEY, MASSACHUSETTS

Detail of Cornice—Built in 1803

THE CABOT-CHURCHILL HOUSE, BRISTOL, RHODE ISLAND

The eagles, one poised over each corner, were carved out of White Pine, according to tradition, by sailors of the
intrepid "Yankee" of which Capt. Churchill was Master

Early American Cornices, Part II

One probable source to which the American builder-architect resorted for motives was unquestionably furniture, either in the executed pieces, or in the catalogs of the various English manufactures; and with furniture must be included mantels, since these were often made by furniture factories and illustrations of them were included in the catalogs. There was at that time a rather curious condition in England; furniture design had long borrowed motives from architecture and much early furniture was designed by architects, but during the latter half of the eighteenth century men who began their careers as cabinet makers became architects, and in the design of houses we find many motives obviously borrowed from furniture design. It is likely then that occasional American architects closely in touch with English work, derived the new motives which suddenly appeared toward the close of the century from English furniture books, and it is likewise probable that the American compilers of architectural books, men like Pain and Asher Benjamin, copied or at least freely transcribed from them. As the Adam brothers were the authors of books on furniture and architectural design, it is quite possible that they influenced American work to an extent that is not realized, by this indirect method, but the date of their publications and work, would seem to indicate that it was rather the books of earlier men that were most used and most useful.

There was another and important factor, and that was the most admirable library possessed by most Colonial builders. This may have been but a single volume, and was probably never more than three or four, but such books as "*Palladio Londiniensis,*" Pain's "*House Carpenter*" and Benjamin's "*Country Builder's Assistant,*" do not exist today. They contained literally all that the Colonial architect needed to know, and what library is there today which gives that and no more? We have too many books, so that our instinctive feeling for design is obscured or thwarted by our conflicting knowledges. The Colonial architect found himself in one strong current of design, easy to swim in because he swam with the current, not across or against it, and because he was powerfully guided and supported by his books; whereas we are directed by our libraries now across and now against the stream, and alas, we not infrequently sink, weighted down by our useless information.

Too high praise cannot be given these colonial books; it is true that not all decorative motives in our early American work are direct copies of plates in them, but it is obvious that with their publication toward the end of the eighteenth century there was an immediate and enormous increase in the number of motives commonly employed, in the use of ornamented moldings and decorated friezes, and in a sort of general release from the genuine (though degraded) classic succession of moldings. It will thus be found that the most interesting of the so-called colonial houses, especially in their detail, date from the years immediately succeeding the Revolution, and before the publication of the archaeological books on Roman and Greek work, like Stuart and Revett's "*Antiquities of Athens.*" Asher Benjamin and Daniel Raynerd's book, "*The American Builder's Companion; or, a NEW SYSTEM OF ARCHITECTURE; Particularly Adapted to The*

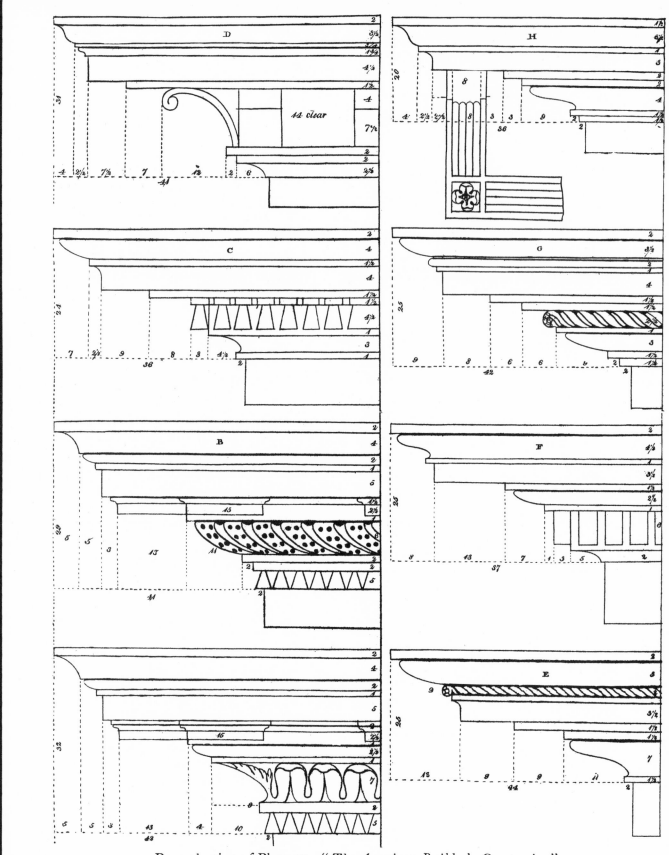

Reproduction of Plate 12—"*The American Builder's Companion*"
By Asher Benjamin. Published at Boston in 1806

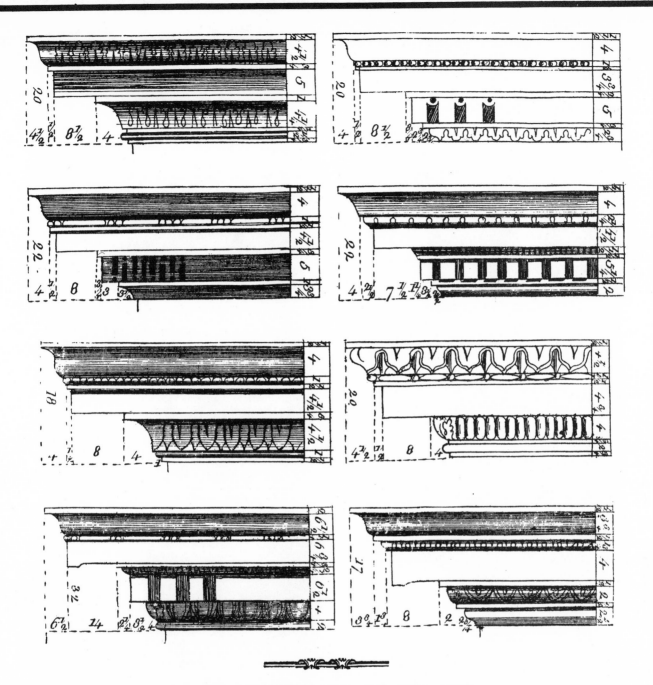

EXPLANATION OF PLATE LIV.

TO proportion the cornice and frize to rooms, or any place required ; give them three fourths of an inch to a foot, including the frize and necking ; fuppofe them to be fourteen feet, more or lefs ; at fourteen feet the cornice and frize, including the necking, will be 10½ inches ; divide that into 12 parts, give 5 to the cornice, 6 to the frize, and one to the necking ; if cornices are ufed without frize or necking, give them three eighths of an inch to a foot, or half an inch to a foot ; fuppofe 14 feet as before, at three eighths of an inch to a foot, the cornice will be 5¼ inches : at half an inch to the foot, the cornice will be 7 inches ; whatever the given height is, that muft be divided into the fame number of parts as the cornice you make ufe of, and difpofe them to the parts in height and projection, as figured on the cornices.

Reproductions of Plates and Text from
PAIN'S "PRACTICAL HOUSE CARPENTER"

Present Style of Building in The United States of America" was published in 1806. In the preface the authors state, "Being the first who have for a great length of time published any New System of Architecture, we do not expect to escape some degree of censure. Old-fashioned workmen, who have for many years followed the footsteps of Palladio and Langley, will, no doubt, leave their old path with great reluctance ...We do not conceive it essentially necessary to adhere exactly to any particular order, provided the proportion and harmony of the parts be carefully preserved. If, for instance in any of the cornices an ovolo should be changed for an ogee, or for a hollow, so trifling an alteration could not destroy the effect of the whole, provided it were done with any degree of judgment."

American artisans shone by comparison with those of other countries, in that they were so free from tradition that they dared to depart from the stereotyped. The cornices of the main house, the window and the porch of the Bacon House at Kent, Connecticut, built in 1810, in all of which dentil courses and consols appear. The porch seems to have been added rather late, since the consols have degenerated into one board set upon another, instead of the molded solid blocks of the older work, while the porch dentils are merely small oblong blocks nailed to the frieze, without intermediate pieces. The same type of dentils are used on the main cornice, the windows and the door and show how interestingly the early builders could vary a motive which had been in use so long as to seem almost impervious to change. The short portion of the frieze is most unusual and well designed for its purpose, the vertical applied members being obviously derived from the triglyph, while the half round between them may be reminiscent of the swag. The native sense of design was usually sufficiently acute to keep the artisans within the bounds of the appropriate.

The dentil course was a favorite motive, but rarely used in its original form. Sometimes it was composed of guttae, often it became a combination of the Greek fret and the dentil and sometimes a row of drops either turned or square.

Another frequently used motive in early American cornices is one for which there is no name, or at least no name in common use; the curious row of curved corbels. The motive is a full cove

used as a cornice, not uncommon in Colonial times; some of the earliest wood buildings in Massachusetts had plaster coves of this shape below the corona, and it remained a common crown motive on the brick and stone buildings around Philadelphia. It has been asserted that the curved consol was derived from the cove cornice. This seems hardly likely in view of the fact that while the motive was not common in England it was by no means unknown, and is frequently found in furniture before 1800; so that it was most likely a transformed furniture design used in architecture. The motive was published here before 1800 and very likely in England also, so that by 1799 when the Pierce house at Portsmouth, New Hampshire, was built it was an accepted part of the architect's repertory. This house, by the way, is attributed to Bulfinch, and while the writer has no facts to support this attribution, the house itself by its correct and mannered design is evidence that it was not the offhand product of some local carpenter-architect, even in a place where the average work was of so excellent a quality.

It is an old adage that the best work has in it something of imperfection, and this is again demonstrated by a comparison with the Pierce house and the Cabot-Churchill house at Bristol, Rhode Island. The latter, built

Detail of Cornice—Built in 1810
THE BACON HOUSE, KENT, CONNECTICUT

Detail of Cornice—Built in 1790
THE OLD PARKER HOUSE, ESSEX, CONNECTICUT

Detail of Entrance Cornice—Built about 1800
THE PRUDENCE CRANDALL HOUSE, CANTERBURY, CONNECTICUT

in 1803, four years after the Pierce house, is far less sophisticated and yet more interesting. One can hardly uphold the railing as a model for copyists, the cymatium is probably too big and the dentil course too small to be perfect in scale, yet the whole cornice possesses a vigorous and insistent individuality rarely found in technically more skillful work. The eagles at the four corners doubtless aid in producing this sensation,

ornament simulating swags. The drops are tapered turned wood pegs nailed to the frieze, with the swags between carved in arcs of a circle; there is no indication of cloth, or of any other material, and yet the general effect is very pleasant, especially as emphasized in the photograph by the excellent leader head. This cornice has practically no soffit, the tight bead ornament below the corona being almost flush with the house, one of

A HOUSE AT SHARON, CONNECTICUT

although they are by no means entirely responsible, even with the pretty legend recited in the caption.

In the last group of houses executed before the Classic Revival superseded the genuine American expression of the Renaissance, we find some very interesting treatments of the frieze below the cornices. The house at Sharon, Connecticut (Fig. 22), is of the simple type with applied wood

the few examples of this kind in the country. The designer of the house at 409 Hope Street, Bristol, Rhode Island, "bit off more than he could chew," when he applied such a mouthful of architecture to the cornice; and his failure to appreciate the necessity of proper scale is the cause of the general bad effect of a cornice which contains some interesting features, notably the swags, and the saw tooth ornament at the bot-

Detail of Cornice—Built in 1799
THE JOHN PIERCE HOUSE, PORTSMOUTH, NEW HAMPSHIRE

THE CHASE HOUSE, NEWBURYPORT, MASSACHUSETTS

tom of the frieze. This saw tooth ornament is quite often found in furniture, especially on the frames of dressers and cupboards, but is exceedingly rare as an architectural ornament; the only other cases where it was used that come to mind being in an exterior door-way in Alexandria, Virginia, and in an interior doorway in Winchester in the Shenandoah Valley.

The house at Chatham Center, New York,

find doorways, window heads and mantels decorated and sometimes over decorated with carved sunbursts, rosettes and flutes all executed with a gouge. In the example illustrated even the urn between the sun rays could readily be cut with a gouge by a carpenter who was in no sense a carver, if he had a good layout of the design on his board.

Another furniture motive is the Chinese Chippendale interlaced fret on the frieze of the Wain-

HOUSE AT 409 HOPE STREET, BRISTOL, RHODE ISLAND

built in 1789 has a frieze ornament borrowed from plaster work, and which, though used in a curious way in this case, was quite a common method of ornamentation around New York City, especially by the workmen of Dutch descent. It was executed by a gouge only, and complicated as it appears, could be carved rapidly and cheaply by a good mechanic (he did not need to be a good carver), so that on many of the Dutch houses we

wright house at Middlebury, Vermont, built in 1807. This was probably cut out with a key-hole saw and applied within a panel; and is especially satisfactory in combination with finely detailed cornice and pilasters, and the St. Andrews cross of the railing.

In the house at Nichols, Tioga County, New York, on a road running along the banks of the Susquehanna River (part of the old trail from the Hudson at Kingston to the headwaters of the Delaware at Unadilla), the decoration of the frieze has really a functional part to play in the design of the facade, in a manner which would make Vignola squirm, but which somehow does not seem at all forced in reality. This is a house of quite late design, with a mantel-like window trim, and though the treatment of the building is very free, it was evidently done by a man who

has perhaps little conscious attempt at personal design, and its variance from book Greek architecture is most likely due to the inability of its builder to read plans, but the "White House" at Charlestown, New Hampshire, is of a different sort. The classic motives appear to have been pretty clearly understood and consciously altered, not out of caprice, but from a realization that the type of triglyph and mutule,

HOUSE AT CHATHAM CENTER, NEW YORK

knew very thoroughly what he was about. By the time this house was built, the American carpenter-architect had learned his business.

Even when what we have agreed to call the Colonial style was finally extinguished by the Greek Revival, the indigenous quality managed to make itself felt through the veneer of Greek forms. The cornice of the Windham Bank at Windham, Connecticut, built in 1832

which was suited to a marble structure with walls three feet thick, might not be appropriate to a wooden house with six-inch walls. Thus in the frieze of the "White House," we have triglyphs of lace-like delicacy and moldings of very small scale, although the classic proportion is pretty closely held.

Before this (at least to the writer) fascinating subject is laid aside a word should be said about the treatment of the gable end. Of course, in many cases, the classic theory of carrying the full cornice up the rake was adhered to, with various degrees of success at the critical point where the raking cornice intersects with the horizontal; but in a much larger number of cases the whole cornice was carried across the front only, with the corona and cymatium returning flush with the gables and the bed molds returning on

cases where he felt that a horizontal line at the cornice height was needed across the gable end, and that a full cornice was too heavy. This he solved in a number of ways, of which perhaps the most interesting was to return the main cornice on itself around the corner of the gable, but with a reduced projection, and carry the bed molds like a band across the gable; a very ingenious and sometimes lovely piece of design.

THE WAINWRIGHT HOUSE, MIDDLEBURY, VERMONT

themselves. In general, it may be said that with slopes of less than 30° the classic method appears to be the better, but for the steep roofs so common in our early work, the flat return is far the best, and in our modern houses of colonial precedent, a repeated error is to return the horizontal cornice across the gable end on all shapes of roof, making a true pediment of bad proportion. Like ourselves, the colonial designer sometimes found

The return of the main cornice on the gable end was always a problem, and the bad solutions we find on most present-day houses not designed by capable architects (and even on some which are), indicate better than words the ability in design of the old craftsmen, although the actual execution often fell behind the conception. As has just been said, the return of the full corince at normal projection across the gables is the exception rather than the rule; the most usual solution was to terminate the cornice somewhere near the corner, between the front and the gable end, finishing the gable end with a rake mold, but the exact point of termination was not fixed by custom. We find many cases where the full cornice was returned for a short distance around the corner, a distance only determined by what the designer considered appropriate unless corner pilasters were used, in which case the edge of the

molds, frieze and architrave returned upon themselves on the front of the building, perhaps with the inside edge of the corner board as a limiting point.

All the above treatments give a shelf upon which the end of the rake molds or verge boards may rest, but there are also many instances where the complete cornice extends as a decorative bank on the front only, returned upon itself

HOUSE AT NICHOLS, TIOGA COUNTY, NEW YORK

ters were used, in which case the edge of the pilaster was naturally the limiting element; we find other cases in which all members of the cornice are returned but with a soffit greatly reduced in width so that the cornice becomes a sort of fragment of the belt course at each corner of the gable end; and perhaps the happiest solution is that in which only the corona and cymatium are returned around the corner with all bed

as close as possible to the corner, but not around it. This left the rake mold (invariably present), to take care of itself at the bottom; a very awkward thing to manage and one which the Colonial architects found too much for them. Sometimes the foot of the rake was cut to the profile of the corona and cymatium and these members butted against it, sometimes the verge board turned at an angle and became the corner board

Detail of Cornice and Pilaster
"THE WHITE HOUSE," CHARLESTOWN, NEW HAMPSHIRE

with the small mold at its top, below the overhanging shingles left in the air at the bottom, and sometimes the two returned around the corner at the front to meet the cornice. This was, of course, possible only with a box gutter and when the slope of the roof intersected the wall line at or near the height of the top of the cornice itself. Some of these methods were only partially successful, but it is undoubtedly true that even the poorest was better than a direct copy of the Classic cornice applied to the wood-built country house.

The illustrations in these articles should be sufficient to prove to the American architect how great a scope even a limited field offers to a man of ideas and imagination. In our present struggle for originality we tend to look to exotic architectures and bizarre motives for precedents, and by copying these things we seek for something new, regardless of its appropriateness to our civilization or our methods of construction. The Colonial architect knew less than we, and perhaps in that was his salvation, for he was forced by his own limitations to express himself within them to the everlasting advantage of his art.

Detail of Cornice
THE WINDHAM BANK, WINDHAM, CONNECTICUT

WINDOW—THE FAIRFAX HOUSE, CAMERON STREET, ALEXANDRIA, VIRGINIA

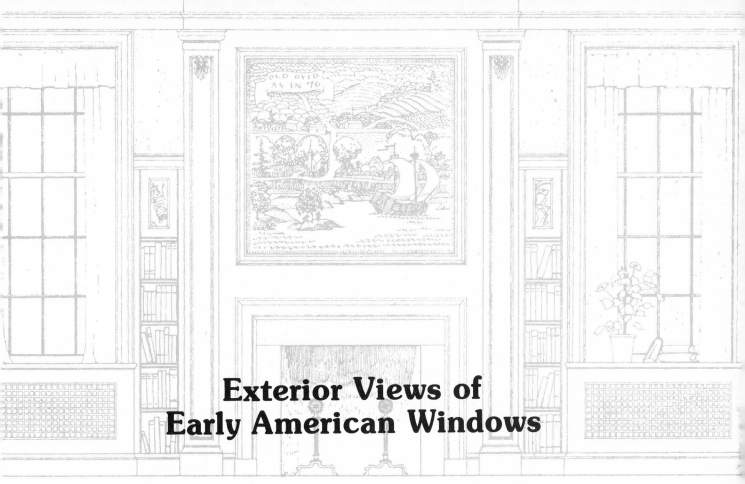

Exterior Views of Early American Windows

ORNAMENTAL features in the early American house were confined to salient points, especially the doors, the cornices, and the windows. Windows naturally need a somewhat slighter degree of decoration than do the doorways; in the first place it is not necessary to mark them for identification as it were, and in the second place, the patterns of the muntins dividing the panes in themselves are an agreeable ornamental feature when their proportion is correct as compared with the sizes of the openings and the mass of the building in which these openings are pierced. It has however been an architectural habit since very early times, and in practically all styles, to introduce some form of decoration in and around the windows. In Gothic architecture, of course, it was the divisions between the windows which became of importance, to the neglect of the wall surrounding them: in the Renaissance period it was the frame of the window that was of importance rather than the window itself, and since our Colonial architecture was derived from that of the Renaissance this decorative treatment of the frame of the opening rather than of the divisions of the openings was the one employed when any ornament at all was thought to be necessary. There are of course exceptions to this; circular headed windows very frequently had interesting tracery motifs used in the divisions of the sash into lights, and transom lights and side lights of doors or triple windows and the circular or semi-circular or elliptical windows in the gable ends were often amusingly divided, so often in fact that certain methods of divi-

sion came to be commonly accepted stock motifs, as for example the "globe" window in the gable ends.

These were however especial cases and for the most part the Colonial architects contented themselves with plain rectangular openings divided into smaller rectangles and decorated, where decoration was attempted, by an ornamental hood, without any change in the architraves of the jambs of the windows and at the sill. In very many of the simpler houses (though not necessarily the smaller ones) no special decorative treatment was attempted and it was rarely that in country houses of stone or brick that any treatment of the hoods or bottoms of the windows for purely decorative purposes was introduced. In these masonry structures the lintel was less common than the flat or segmental arch, sometimes with stone key blocks and occasionally with a plain brick key block; in stone houses brick arches were very frequently used to support the walls above, the centering of these arches being a heavy oak beam left in place. For the most part, however, the earlier houses were of wood and the windows were framed with a simple architrave, either molded or plain with a hood extending across the head and returning upon itself at the ends. This hood was in practically all cases derived from the classic cornice, sometimes being only the cymatium, sometimes the full cornice and sometimes a frieze and cornice which together with the architrave gives a full entablature. Once in a while the window was treated with a motive derived from the full order,

133

WINDOW—JUDGE LEE HOUSE, CAMBRIDGE, MASSACHUSETTS

although in the Bacon house at Kent, Connecticut, the pilasters at the side are indicated only and actually do not exist.

Since practically all Colonial houses have blinds or shutters on the exterior, the treatment of the architraves or jambs was obviously of little importance. The blinds when open covered this portion of the window completely and as a matter of fact a pilaster would have been a nuisance rather than a help because of its interference with the swing of the blind unless reduced to a very flat projection. The heads were usually horizontal and the great variety of interesting treatments which our Colonial ancestors discovered for this simple feature is remarkable unless we remember the extreme freedom with which they varied traditional cornice forms and consider that the heads of the windows are after all cornices in miniature. Take for example the Bacon house and the Strong house. In the Strong house, a triglyph is suggested by the application of half-round molding of various lengths with the ends cut off, while in the Bacon house we have a sort of dentil course running half way down the frieze and the corona and the cymatium of the cornice broken and covered in an amusing and picturesque manner, unprecedented in Renaissance work although obviously suggested by the breaks of the cornices over the columns or pilasters in certain forms of Renaissance wall treatment. These architects did not, however, stop at horizontal hoods; pediments, broken pediments, and scroll pediments, were familiar to them, those in the Wolcott House at Litchfield, Connecticut, and the Pepperill House Saco, Maine, approaching the classic form very closely, while the broken pediment of the Moulton House at Hampton, New Hampshire, could only exist in the early architecture of the United States although its genesis is clearly to be seen. We have here an approximation to the classic scroll pediment with a pineapple in the center so familiar in Georgian work, but here with the scrolls meeting and the pineapple (translated into an acorn) hung from a point in the junction of the scrolls rather than standing upright between them.

Our architects however were by no means limited to a single motive. In the Vernon house the walls of which are of wood carved to imitate stone, the head was fashioned in a manner reminiscent of the flat stone arch and in The Old Manse at Suffield, Connecticut a sort of double key block of wood is inserted in the middle of the head trim, a variation of wooden architecture obvi-

THE KNEELAND HOUSE, HARTFORD, VERMONT

The illustrated window, taken from
the Harriett Lane House (about 1802) in
Windsor, Vt., is carefully proportioned to the
house as a whole and delicately ornamented
with an Adam-like entablature.

THE PEPPERELL HOUSE, SACO, MAINE

THE BELL HOUSE, MORAVIAN SEMINARY, BETHLEHEM, PA.

ously derived from stone, and in the Jessup house a rather late example, we have a combination of the pilaster trim with panel backs and a flat head trim surmounted by an arch form consisting merely of a molding with flush boards in the semicircle to distinguish it from the shingle walls of the building. In the Ruggles house at Columbia Falls, Maine, the walls are entirely of flush boards with sawn wood pieces applied to these boards in imitation of the familiar cloth swags of Empire design.

The treatment of the heads of the windows has however very little effect upon the appearance of the house as a whole unless they project so far as to cast very large and distinct shadows. An observant architect may have often passed a Colonial house which he admires extremely without noticing the treatment of the heads of the windows at all, and this because the pattern of the muntins against the dark of the window is so much more strongly marked than the lighter and more delicate shadows cast by the window heads; and it is likely that in most of our modern imitations of Colonial work the failure to reproduce the Colonial characteristics arises more often from a bad division of the window opening than from any other cause except a fundamental un-Colonial mass form of the building. There is also a very real and important connection in Colonial between the division of the openings and the shape of the structure in which they occur; whether this is because we are accustomed to seeing certain types of sash correspond to houses of certain shapes, or whether it is because there is a positive relation between the two is difficult to say. It is however certain that the early houses were of a different mass than the later ones, that the lights of glass were smaller and that the muntins

WINDOW—HOUSE AT NORWICH, VERMONT

WOLCOTT HOUSE, LITCHFIELD, CONNECTICUT

HOUSE AT EAST HARTFORD, CONNECTICUT

were heavier. It has often been stated (probably with truth) that the shapes of the old windows were determined by the sizes of the glass available. We know that large panes were impossible to obtain in the colonies before the beginning of the 17th century and very difficult to obtain until about the time of the Revolutionary war. Likewise the later craftsmen discovered better practices of woodworking, and endeavoring to keep the muntins to a minimum width, reduced them to sizes which are difficult for our mills to follow today. The early muntins averaged perhaps an inch in width whereas the later ones rarely exceed five-eights of an inch and were occasionally as thin as one-half an inch so that the earlier windows, had a feeling of strength compared with an almost spider web lightness of the muntins in the house at Waldens Bridge, New York. It must not be assumed that there was any sharp division of practice at any given date, the sections of the country were at that time far more separated than is today the case and the practice of any craftsmanship was dependent upon the tradition of the neighborhood to an extent that will never again be the case. It was about at the middle of the eighteenth century that in the large centers of population a very decided change in the quality of craftsmanship was taking place, while in the remoter parts of the country the earlier practices were still obtained; we have for example in the little town of Clinton, Georgia, and in the outskirts of Chilicothe, Ohio, houses which should be dated 1750 instead of 1820 so far as their methods of design and of construction go. The Colonial tradition still lived in these remote districts when the Greek revival had overwhelmed the older style in New York and Boston.

It is a remarkable thing that this Colonial architecture of ours so limited in its materials, so hampered by the great cost of labor as compared with wealth of the day, produced so many and such interesting variances from tradition. It may indeed have been that the factors which we assume to have been hampering ones were actually those which produced its quality. Conklin, the biologist, in his discussion of heredity and environment, says that in our struggle to improve the environment of the American people we have forgotten that we do not know what is the proper environment. Lincoln, for example, born to a life of ease, would certainly not have been the Lincoln he was, and it is certainly possible or indeed most probable that given a "better environment" he would have been a less useful man. So with our architecture.

"THE SYCAMORES,"
SOUTH HADLEY, MASSACHUSETTS

GEN. STRONG HOUSE, VERGENNES, VERMONT

WINDOW—MASONIC LODGE ROOM,
NEW BERN, NORTH CAROLINA

GEN. MOULTON HOUSE, HAMPTON, NEW HAMPSHIRE

MEETING HOUSE NEAR HOPEWELL, BUCKS COUNTY, PA.

WARHAM WILLIAMS HOUSE, NORTHFORD, CONNECTICUT

HOUSE AT WALDENS BRIDGE, NEW YORK

THE VAN COURTLANDT MANSION, NEW YORK, N.Y.

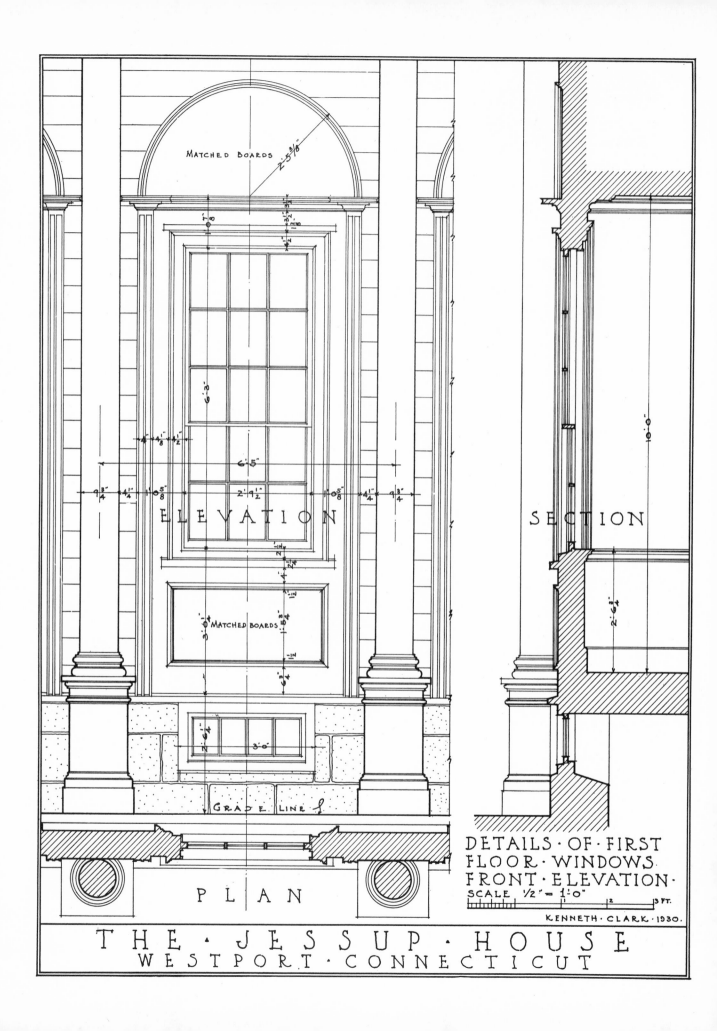

MATCHED BOARDS

2'-5 3/8"

ELEVATION

SECTION

MATCHED BOARDS

GRADE LINE

PLAN

DETAILS · OF · FIRST
FLOOR · WINDOWS ·
FRONT · ELEVATION ·
SCALE 1/2" = 1'-0"

3 FT.

KENNETH · CLARK · 1930.

THE · JESSUP · HOUSE
WESTPORT · CONNECTICUT

THE JESSUP HOUSE, WESTPORT, CONNECTICUT

WINDOW DETAILS—LIVING ROOM
THE JAMES BRICE HOUSE
ANNAPOLIS, MARYLAND

MEASURED DRAWINGS *from*
The George F. Lindsay Collection

INTERIOR ELEVATION OF LIVING ROOM WINDOW

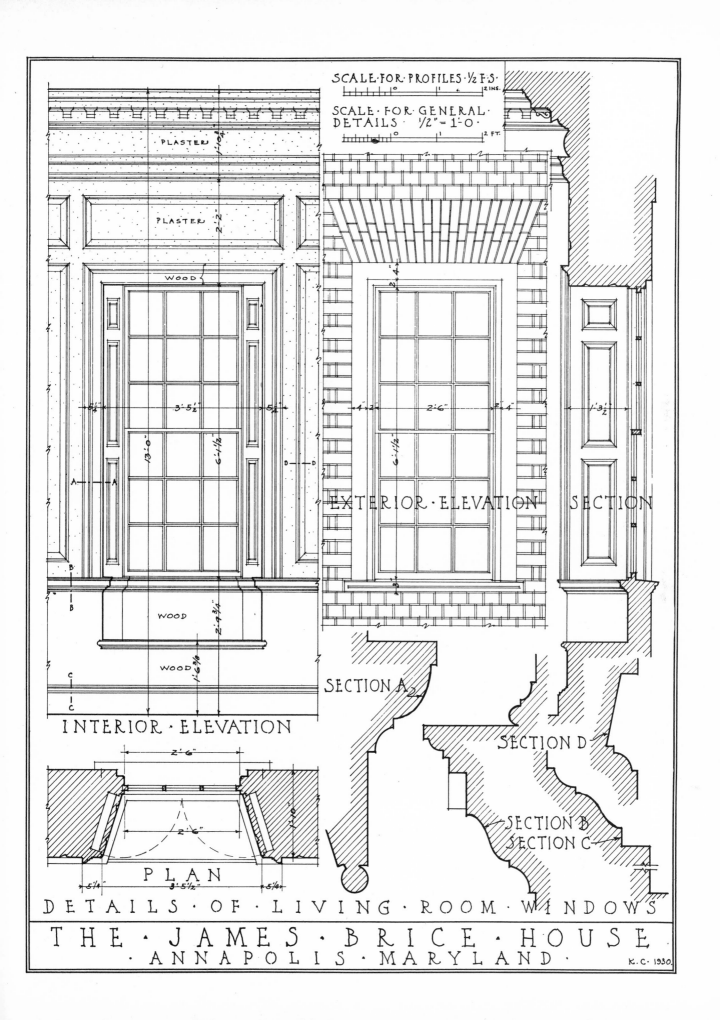

SCALE·FOR·PROFILES·½·F·S·

SCALE·FOR·GENERAL·
DETAILS·½"=1'·0·

PLASTER

PLASTER

WOOD

WOOD

WOOD

WOOD

INTERIOR·ELEVATION

EXTERIOR·ELEVATION

SECTION

PLAN

SECTION A

SECTION D

SECTION B
SECTION C

DETAILS·OF·LIVING·ROOM·WINDOWS

THE·JAMES·BRICE·HOUSE
·ANNAPOLIS·MARYLAND·

K·C·1930·

THE COL. ROBERT MEANS HOUSE, AMHERST, NEW HAMPSHIRE

THE VERNON HOUSE, NEWPORT, RHODE ISLAND

DETAIL OF WINDOW — THE OLD MANSE
Built in Suffield, Connecticut in 1742

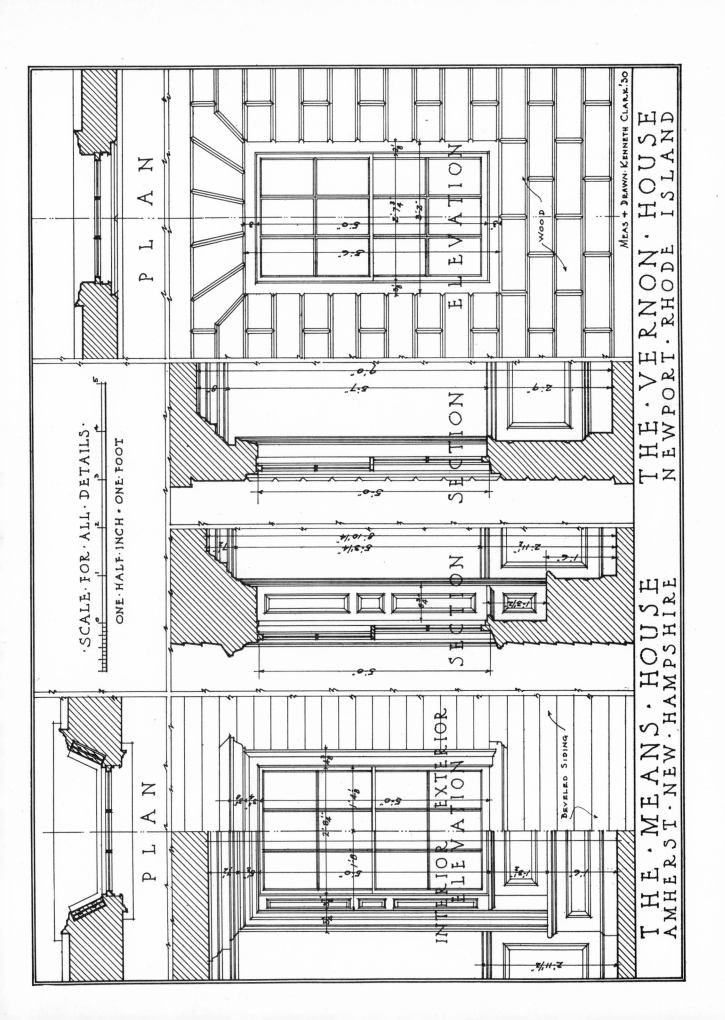

PLAN

ELEVATION

WOOD

SECTION

SECTION

SCALE·FOR·ALL·DETAILS·

ONE·HALF·INCH·ONE·FOOT

INTERIOR·ELEVATION

EXTERIOR·ELEVATION

BEVELED SIDING

PLAN

MEAS + DRAWN·KENNETH CLARK·'30

THE·VERNON·HOUSE
NEWPORT·RHODE·ISLAND

THE·MEANS·HOUSE
AMHERST·NEW·HAMPSHIRE

JOHN VOGLER HOUSE, WINSTON-SALEM, NORTH CAROLINA

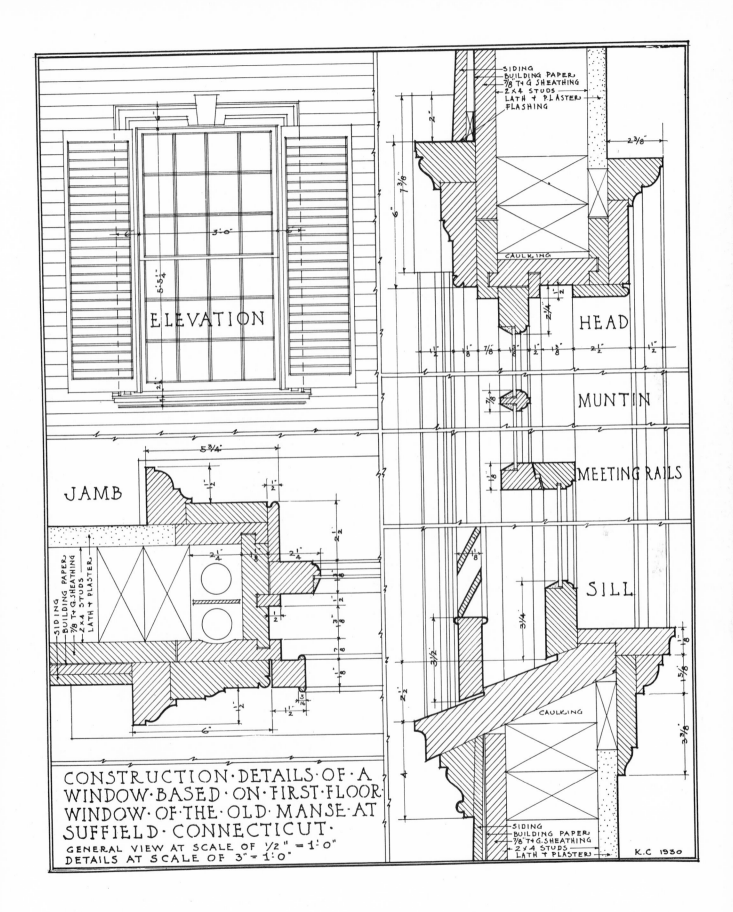

ELEVATION

HEAD

MUNTIN

MEETING RAILS

SILL

JAMB

SIDING
BUILDING PAPER
7/8" T+G SHEATHING
2×4 STUDS
LATH + PLASTER
FLASHING

CAULKING

SIDING
BUILDING PAPER
7/8" T+G SHEATHING
2×4 STUDS
LATH + PLASTER

SIDING
BUILDING PAPER
7/8" T+G SHEATHING
2×4 STUDS
LATH + PLASTER

CAULKING

CONSTRUCTION·DETAILS·OF·A·
WINDOW·BASED·ON·FIRST·FLOOR·
WINDOW·OF·THE·OLD·MANSE·AT·
SUFFIELD·CONNECTICUT·
GENERAL VIEW AT SCALE OF 1/2" = 1'·0"
DETAILS AT SCALE OF 3" = 1'·0"

K.C 1930

VESTIBULE, THE PENNIMAN-STEARNS HOUSE, BEDFORD, MASSACHUSETTS
Reuben Duren, Architect

Early American Vestibules

There is one important detail of the old Colonial house, that is rather seldom utilized by modern architects when designing a dwelling in this style —and that is the vestibule entrance, as distinct from the more conventional entrance porch. The rather late type of doorway, with side lights, under a narrow porch, is used over and over again; but the modern house designer has rather strangely overlooked the very practical projecting entrance vestibule found on many houses of early New England architecture, generally indicating a date earlier than the more open porch treatment with columns.

Yet this type of vestibule possesses a most practical means of enlarging a house plan, at precisely that point where it is often most crowded, and in the simplest and most economical way!

Probably it originally took shape from the need of meeting the demand for a larger entrance hall, with more space between entrance door and staircase. Particularly with the typical early Colonial stairway, placed against the front face of the large central chimney, the resulting passageway between the front room doors upon the first floor plan often became both narrow and crowded. When open, the door edge almost brushed the face of the stair run,—and there was little room to greet entering neighbors, particularly if they were to be welcomed within the room on that side of the house where the front door was hinged!

It was probable also that, despite the fact that the early houses were usually built with their entrance sides facing the south; this single doorway, opening directly into the front hall at the foot of the main stairs, was found to cool off the passage between the main front rooms of the house, upon both floors— especially when the house plan was changed to more nearly face the east or west; as came so frequently later to be the case.

We have also the early meeting house plan, with its one or two story vestibule—often inclosing the staircase as well—which was usually first treated as a gabled projection in its exterior handling;—until it came to be taken into the lower stories of the tower with spire, that came into general use at about the period of the building of the "Old North," or Christ Church of Boston. Here this "vestibule" type of entrance treatment had already taken a definitive form of expression—as is indicated by the original brick side vestibule upon the Old South Meeting House.

And so it was an easy step to widen the passageway across the front of the entrance hall, by taking out the front wall between the two posts that always supported the heavy timbers that framed the central chimney, and moving the doorway and wall forward some three to four feet, then filling in the two sides back to the main wall face of the house, and roofing it over either with a ridge roof forming a pediment gable upon the vestibule face, or with a simple hip roof treatment, the latter being often more appropriate to the older and simpler type of early house design.

VESTIBULE—25 FLINT STREET
SALEM, MASSACHUSETTS

In a large majority of instances, these entrance house vestibules were a later addition or alteration made to an older house plan. It is very rarely indeed that it can be indisputably proved that this sort of vestibule was original to the Colonial plan! Usually it is obviously a later afterthought, added to the plan to make it more habitable for the occupants during the colder seasons of the year. And it was almost always added to secure additional needed space within the hall itself. It was very rarely filled with inside coat closets;

In the Bedford house, indeed, the two-story vestibule shown upon the house was added apparently for the purpose of securing a small, narrow staircase from the side door to the upper story; which stairway mounts steeply along the rear or righthand side of the vestibule, over small first floor closets, to the floor above. But this is an exceptional example, with a very rarely used two-story height for this feature, found in a rather late house plan.

The one factor of the outer vestibule that often deceives the casual observer is the entrance doorway, which is generally very obviously old. And it often does not occur to one to think how easily the old doorway (and in fact, whole front wall of the hallway, between the two upright posts) could be cut out and moved forward, to secure the wider hallway,— and that exactly in the single space where this enlargement of the plan was alone desired;—and where it could be easily secured, without causing the

slightest change in anything in the rest of the house.

Sometimes the line where the old plaster was joined to the new wall on the inside of the side walls, shows up very distinctly. Sometimes it is entirely lost because of the manner in which the new side walls of the vestibule are finished around and up to the two main house wall posts that are found placed in these locations. Occasionally, in houses built later than 1780 or 1800, these vestibules may have been part of the original house design; but when found on any building earlier than these dates, there is usually reason to doubt that the vestibule is as old as the house.

Sometimes, in tearing down or altering an old house, the attachment of these vestibules to the house, and particularly in their under-floor and roof construction, becomes definite and plain. The basement wall usually runs right across the space under the vestibule floor, with its exterior underpinning plainly in view. The floor sill, also, is found to butt up against the exterior face of the original house sill, and the plates and rafters are clearly placed against the upper part of the exterior wall face,—often without even removing the clapboards or wall boarding. In these cases there can be no doubt. In the old Dillaway-Thomas house in Roxbury, for instance, built in 1750-52, the side entrance vestibule was added later, probably in 1832, when other changes were known to have been made in the dwelling at the time that it came first into the possession of the Dillaway family.

This supplies a good average date for the change or addition of this outer vestibule to be made. Many

VESTIBULE—HOUSE AT GLOUCESTER
CAPE ANN, MASSACHUSETTS

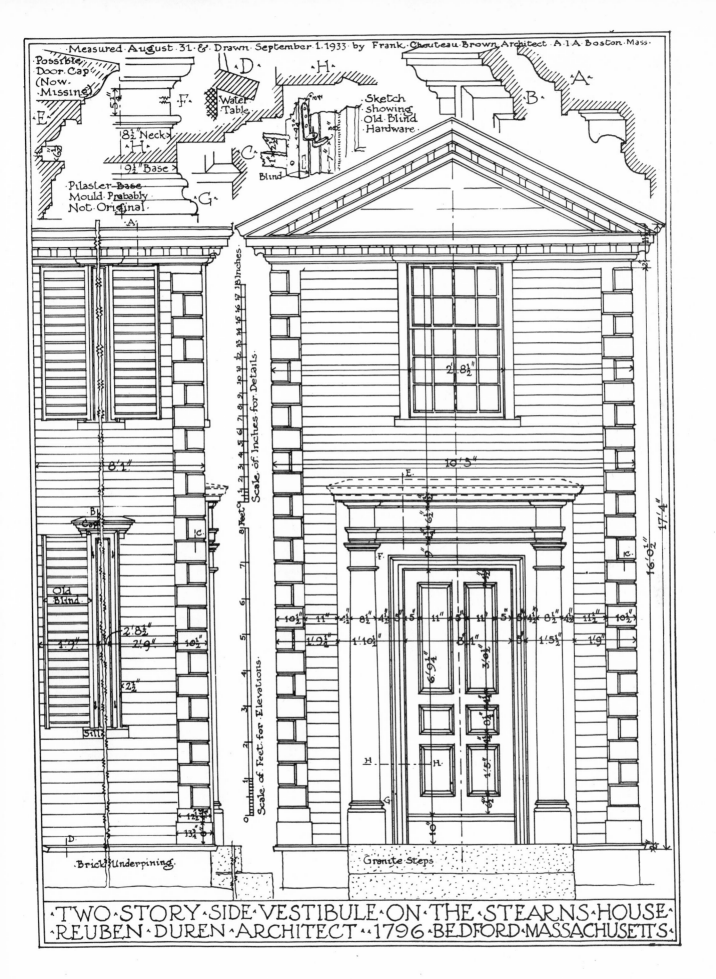

Measured August 31 & Drawn September 1. 1933 by Frank Chouteau Brown Architect A.I.A. Boston Mass.

Possible Door Cap (Now Missing)

E

Water Table

D

H

Sketch showing Old Blind Hardware

A

B

8½" Neck

9½" Base

Blind

Pilaster Base Mould Probably Not Original

G

C

A

F

Scale of Inches for Details.

2'.8½"

10'.3"

Old Blind

B Cap

C

E

F

16'.0½"

17'.4"

C

8'.1"

Scale of Feet for Elevations.

2'.8½"
2'.9"
1'.9"
10½"

10½" 11" 8½" 5 5 11" 5 11" 5 8½" 11½" 10½"

1'.9½" 1'.10½" 8'.1" 1'.5½" 1'.9"

6'.9¼

3'.0¼

5'.11"

2½"

H

H

1'.5"

G

Brick Underpining.

Granite Steps

·TWO·STORY·SIDE·VESTIBULE·ON·THE·STEARNS·HOUSE·
·REUBEN·DUREN·ARCHITECT··1796·BEDFORD·MASSACHUSETTS·

155

VESTIBULE—HOUSE ON BRIDGE STREET
SALEM, MASSACHUSETTS

houses apparently have experienced this change from some time between 1805-10 and 1830-40. It appears then to have been a current fashion in modernization, that came into vogue at about that time,—just a little before the craze for marble Italian mantels which caused them to be imported in such large numbers, and substituted for the earlier and more delicate wooden mantels that had preceded them.

It may be stated that most outside entrance vestibules now to be found on early Colonial houses are of later date than the structures themselves; and this date of change is often extremely difficult to find.

These entrance vestibules also—as is equally true of other architectural details—usually develop marked local characteristics. In and about Salem, for instance, the vestibule ornamented at the corner angle by a rather heavy fluted Doric pilaster, without entasis, is the prevailing type. Possibly the side entrance to the well known Pierce-Johannot-Nichols House in Salem, attributed to McIntire, may have been the original, that was so often copied (some in very recent times!) by other builders, with a few easily managed modifications, all of classic conventionality of handling. In Gloucester a quite different type; wider, shallower; with side and arched toplights, seems to be the prevailing mode. In Marblehead a taller, narrower, more picturesque and informal sort of composition, indicates the less formal character of life and conditions

then in vogue in that town. Andover has developed a vestibule type with square side windows set within an arch or impost motive of classical derivation. On Cape Cod a simple narrow flat pilaster, single or paired, is the prevailing style of vestibule door enframement; and every other district or town center now exhibits its chosen local variation.

And so it goes. Outer projecting vestibules are found in a few earlier dwellings, such as the Col. Paul Wentworth Mansion at Salmon Falls, New Hampshire, built about 1701; or the old Cooper-Austin House in Cambridge, of some forty years earlier date (1657). And while these houses show vestibules of the simplest hipped-roof type; yet they are both of probably much later date than the structures to which they are now found attached.

The simplest types were of course most appropriate to these earlier Tudor pitched roof dwellings,—just as the later, more ornate designs, with pedimented and ornamented face, or balustraded roof treatment, are usually found attached to houses of 1810 to 1825, where it is quite probable that they may have been a part of the original plan and construction. And the same might be said of those more delicately molded and ornamented extensions, such as the two vestibules from Gloucester, one with the leaded glass side and top lights, that equally announce a similar date for their workmanship. In this case, the entire entrance was changed, probably to admit more light to the stairway hall, as well as to secure added space in the hall passage in front of the stairs.

VESTIBULE—HOUSE AT 121 BRIDGE STREET
SALEM, MASSACHUSETTS

VESTIBULE—HOUSE AT 52 ESSEX STREET, SALEM, MASSACHUSETTS

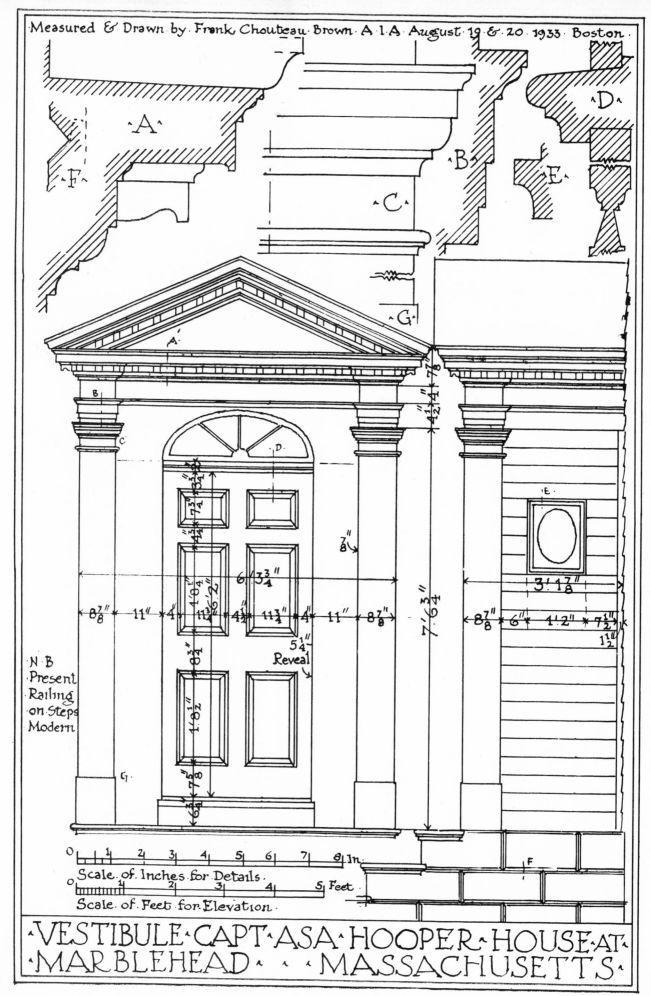

Measured & Drawn by Frank Chouteau Brown A.I.A August 19 & 20 1933 Boston

·A·
·F·
·B·
·C·
·D·
·E·
·G·

·A·
·B·
·C·
·D·
·E·

N·B
Present
Railing
on Steps
Modern

Reveal

0 1 2 3 4 5 6 7 8 In.
Scale. of Inches for Details.

0   1   2   3   4   5 Feet
Scale. of Feet for Elevation.

·VESTIBULE·CAPT·ASA·HOOPER·HOUSE·AT·
·MARBLEHEAD· · ·MASSACHUSETTS·

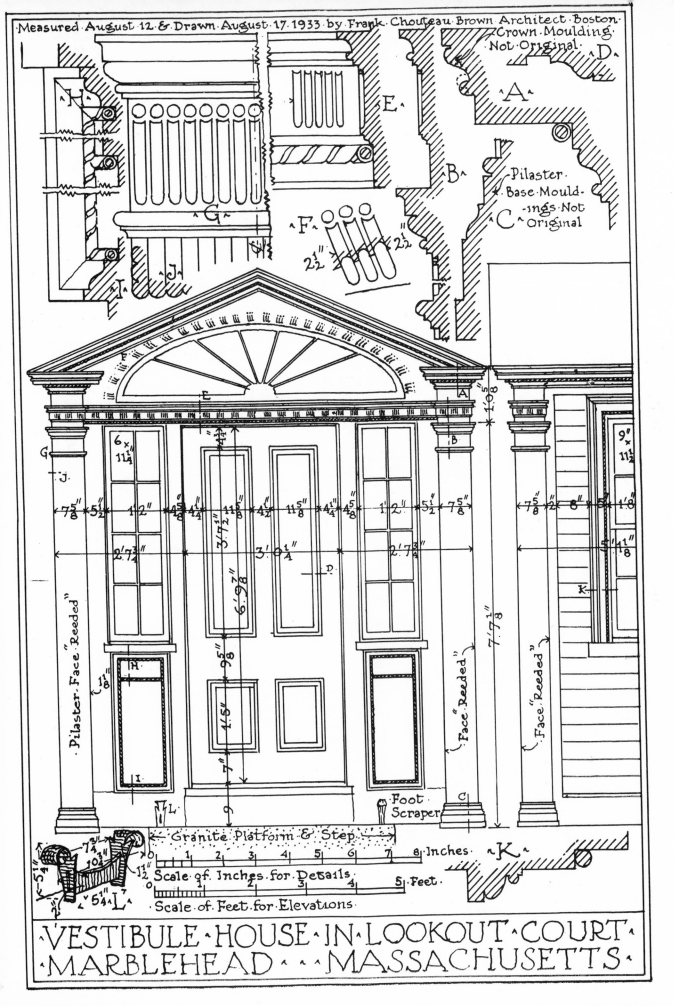

Measured August 12 & Drawn August 17 1933 by Frank Chouteau Brown Architect Boston

Crown Moulding Not Original

Pilaster Base Mould-ings Not Original

VESTIBULE·HOUSE·IN·LOOKOUT·COURT·
MARBLEHEAD·· · ·MASSACHUSETTS

VESTIBULE—CAPT. ASA HOOPER HOUSE
MARBLEHEAD, MASSACHUSETTS

VESTIBULE—HOUSE IN LOOKOUT COURT
MARBLEHEAD, MASSACHUSETTS

HOUSE ON WASHINGTON SQUARE
SALEM, MASSACHUSETTS

DOUBLE VESTIBULE—JUDGE HOLTEN HOUSE, 1670
DANVERS CENTER, MASSACHUSETTS

Measured & Drawn September 10 & 12 1933 by Frank Chouteau Brown Architect

·A·
·B·
·C·
·D·
·E·
·F·

G1.
10 5/8" ×
17 1/4"

Scale of Feet for Elevations.

Scale of Inches for Details.

·SIDE·VESTIBULE·WASHINGTON·SQUARE·
·SALEM· MASSACHUSETTS·

162

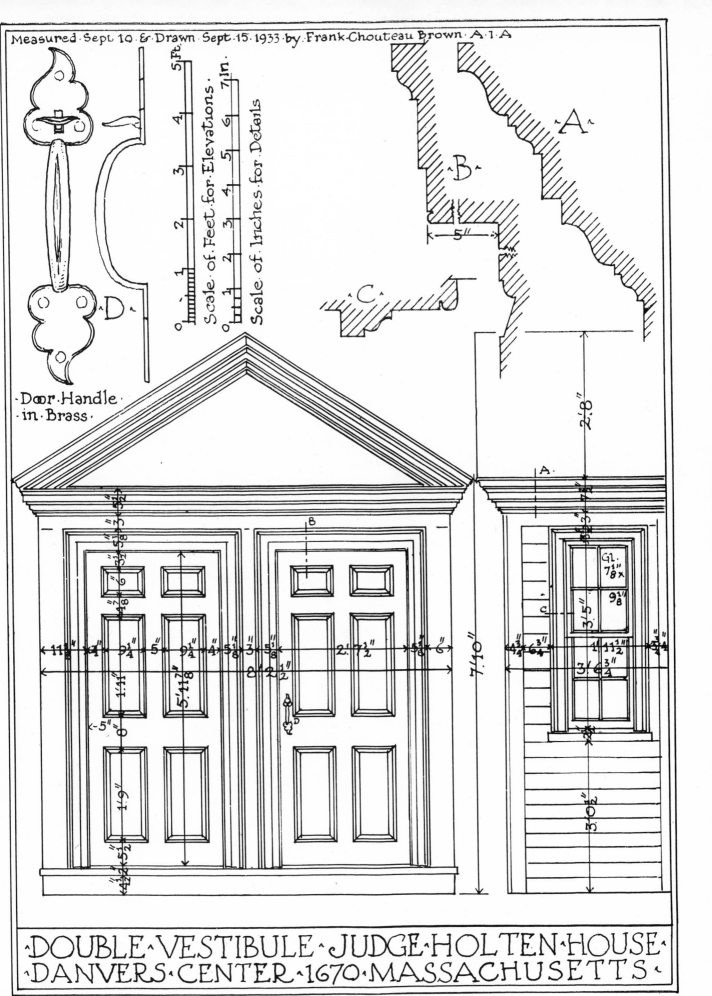

Measured Sept 10 & Drawn Sept 15 1933 by Frank Chouteau Brown A.I.A

Scale of Feet for Elevations.

Scale of Inches for Details.

·A·

·B·

·C·

·Door·Handle·
·in·Brass·

·D·

·DOUBLE·VESTIBULE·JUDGE·HOLTEN·HOUSE·
·DANVERS·CENTER·1670·MASSACHUSETTS·

VESTIBULE—HOUSE AT 26 NORMAN STREET
SALEM, MASSACHUSETTS

VESTIBULE—SAMUEL BROCKELBANK HOUSE—1670
GEORGETOWN, MASSACHUSETTS

VESTIBULE—HOUSE, NO. 23 SUMMER STREET
SALEM, MASSACHUSETTS

VESTIBULE—PEIRCE-NICHOLS HOUSE—1782—SAMUEL McINTIRE
SALEM, MASSACHUSETTS

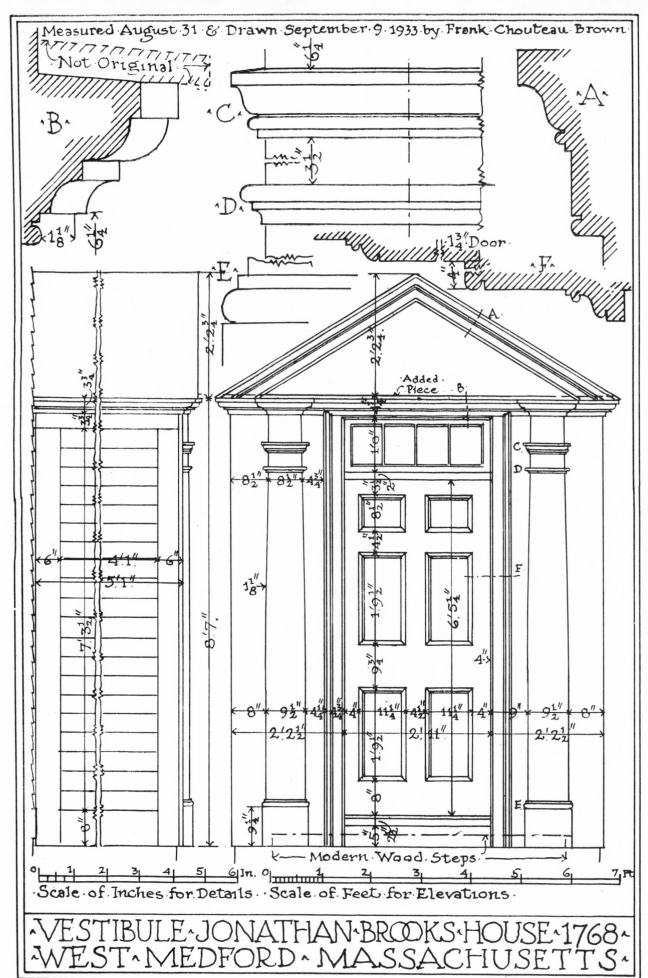

Measured August 31 & Drawn September 9 1933 by Frank Chouteau Brown

Not Original

·B·   ·C·   ·A·

·D·

·E·

1⅛" 6¼"

1'1¾" Door   ·F·

·A·

Added Piece   B

·C·
·D·

·E·

·E·

Modern Wood Steps

0 1 2 3 4 5 6 In.   0 1 2 3 4 5 6 7 Ft
·Scale·of·Inches·for·Details·   ·Scale·of·Feet·for·Elevations·

·VESTIBULE·JONATHAN·BROOKS·HOUSE·1768·
·WEST·MEDFORD·MASSACHUSETTS·

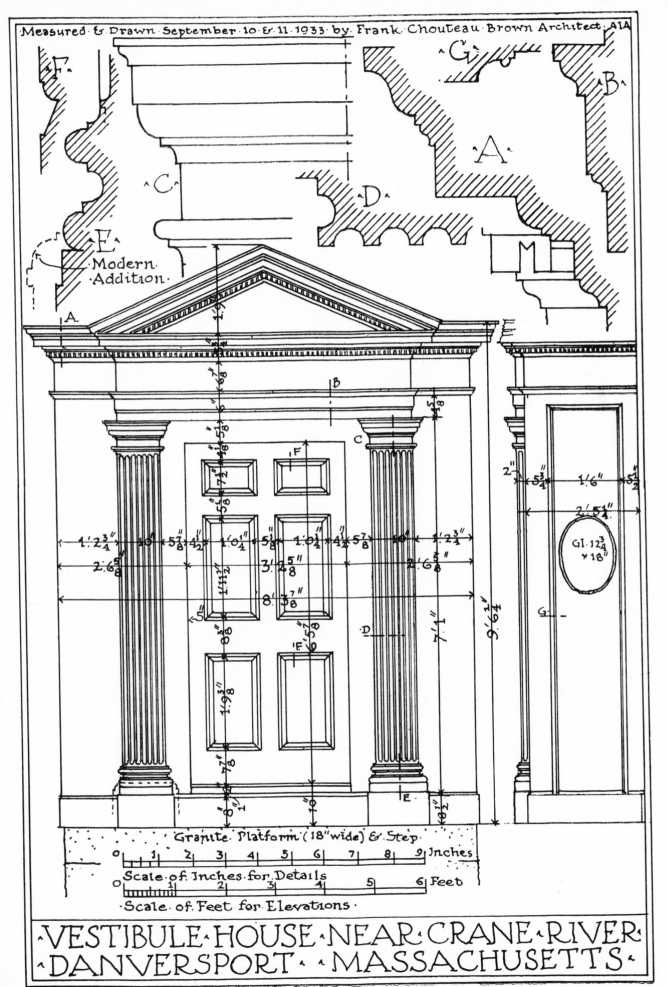

Measured & Drawn September 10 & 11 1933 by Frank Chouteau Brown Architect AIA

Modern Addition.

Granite Platform (18" wide) & Step.

0 1 2 3 4 5 6 7 8 9 Inches
Scale of Inches for Details

0 1 2 3 4 5 6 Feet
Scale of Feet for Elevations.

·VESTIBULE·HOUSE·NEAR·CRANE·RIVER·
·DANVERSPORT· ·MASSACHUSETTS·

VESTIBULE—JONATHAN BROOKS HOUSE—1768
WEST MEDFORD, MASSACHUSETTS

VESTIBULE—HOUSE NEAR CRANE RIVER
DANVERSPORT, MASSACHUSETTS

VESTIBULE—HOUSE ON MIDDLE STREET
GLOUCESTER, CAPE ANN, MASSACHUSETTS

VESTIBULE—WHITTEMORE HOUSE—1760
TOWN HALL SQUARE, GLOUCESTER, MASSACHUSETTS

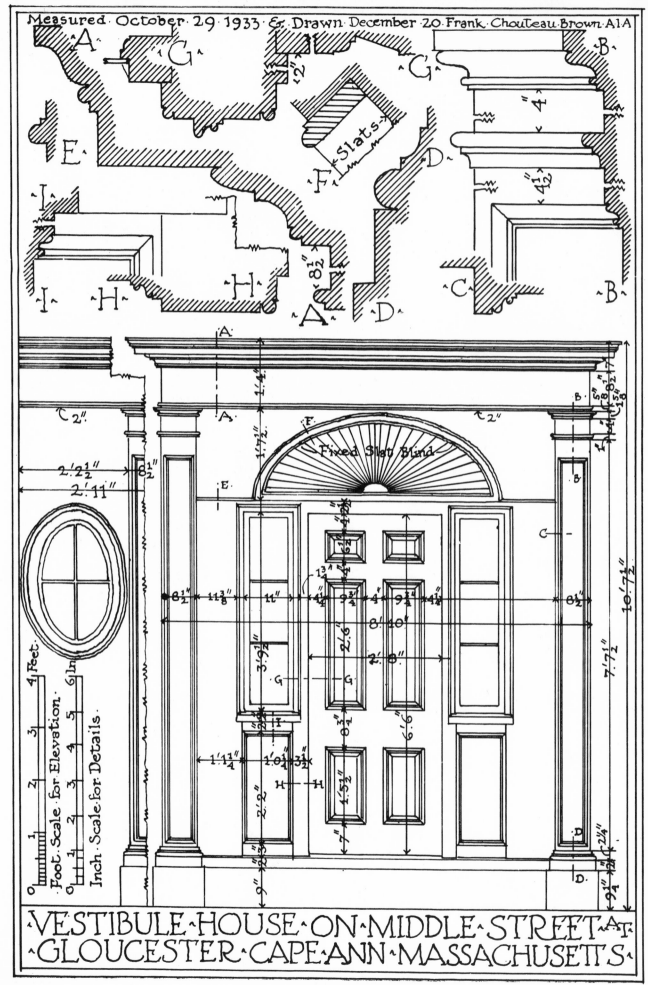

Measured October 29 1933 & Drawn December 20 Frank Chouteau Brown A.I.A

Fixed Slat Blind

Foot Scale for Elevation.
Inch Scale for Details.

VESTIBULE·HOUSE·ON·MIDDLE·STREET·AT·
GLOUCESTER·CAPE·ANN·MASSACHUSETTS·

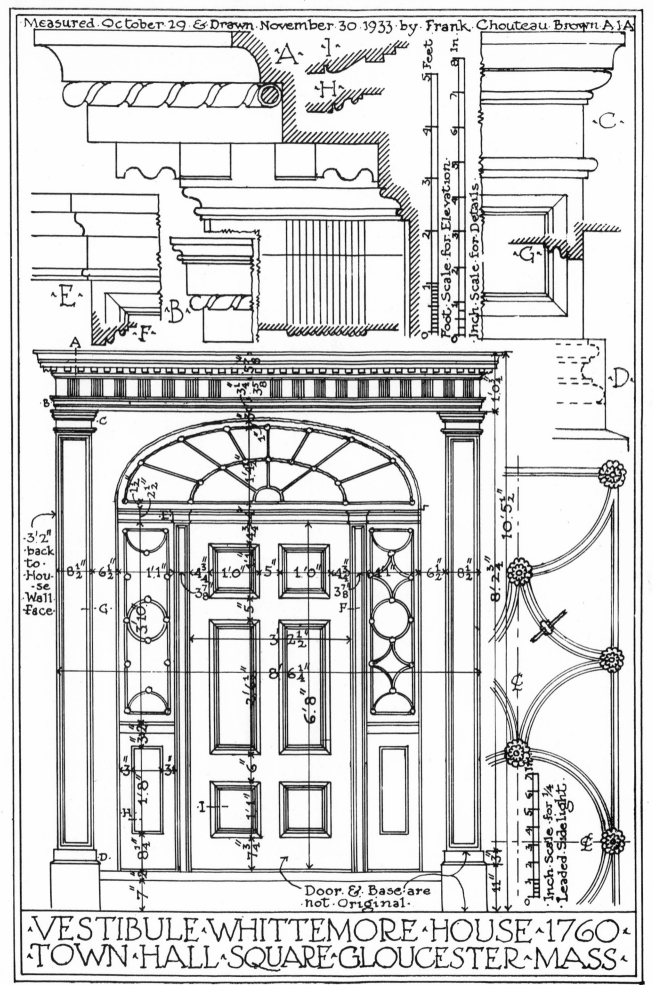

Measured October 29 & Drawn November 30 1933 by Frank Chouteau Brown A.I.A.

·A· ·I·
·H·

·C·

·G·

·E·

·B·

·F·

Foot Scale for Elevation.

Inch Scale for Details.

·D·

A

B

·C·

3'2" back to Hou- se Wall Face

·G·

3'10"

8½" 6½" 1'1" 4¾ 3¾ 1'0" 5 1'0" 4½ 3⅞ 4'1" 6½" 8½"
3⅞

3'2¼"

8'6¼"

6'8"

2'6¼"

1'6"

1'8"

·H·

3 3¼

·I·

8¼ 8¾

7 ¾ 7¼

7'¾

10'5½"

8'2¾"

·C·

·E·

Door & Base are not Original.

Inch Scale for ¼ Leaded Sidelight.

Doorway with Oval Toplight in Entrance Hall
EDWARD CARRINGTON HOUSE—C.1811—PROVIDENCE, RHODE ISLAND

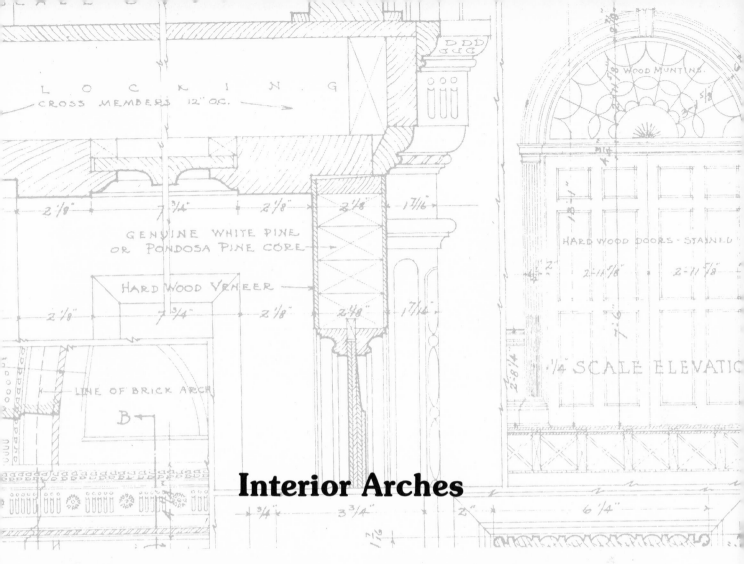

Interior Arches

THE use of the arch form as interior decorative detail executed in wood, while not exactly frequent in New England, nevertheless seems to have been employed quite often—particularly in those houses having the most architectural importance. To be of any magnitude, it is perforce limited to houses of an unusually high stud, especially when used to span wider distances, or when employed in anything approaching a semi-circular form. Its most frequent early uses were, perhaps, in the upper part of the corner cupboard, but it was also sometimes used for interior doorways—as in the Warner House at Portsmouth— 1722. Sometimes these archways were filled with glazed doors or sash, as in the double doorway from the Lee-Nichols House in Cambridge; or the upper part of the wall cupboard from the Elisha Smith House, in Stillwater, Rhode Island. More pretentious toplight examples are the elaborately glazed arched opening in the George Read, II, House, from New Castle, Delaware, or the Doorway in the Music Room of the John Brown House at Providence.

The circular or elliptical cross-Hall archway—especially in the Southeastern coastal regions—has always

been a favorite employment, either to suggest a separation of a rear from a front continuous hallway; to set apart a recess containing a stairway from the main open hall—though with less frequency of use—for an opening between a hall and a main first floor room, or even to partly join or connect a front and a rear parlor.

In demarking a staircase recess, it has even been used in a doubled form, as in Gunston Hall, Fairfax County, Virginia and in the entrance hallway of "Tulip Hill," Anne Arundel County, Maryland. In yet another southern mansion, Wye House, in Talbot County, Maryland, flattened and elliptical arched top openings were used in several instances—along the Hallway, as well as between adjoining rooms.

In the George Read, II, house at New Castle, Delaware not only was the hallway interrupted along its length by two large and elaborately decorated semi-circular archways; but a number of richly patterned glass toplights were used to fill arched openings extending over the wide doorways between interior rooms, as well as above the entrance. These interior doors with arched toplights might be considered even as an endeavor to both "have one's cake and eat it too"; to secure the richness of the arch

ARCHWAY TO PARLOR EXTENSION AS REMODELED ABOUT 1799
HUNTINGTON HOUSE—1752—HADLEY, MASSACHUSETTS

DRAWING ROOM END, WITH ARCHED RECESSES TO FRONT PARLOR
"ELMWOOD"—1760—CAMBRIDGE, MASSACHUSETTS

DINING ROOM END, SHOWING CENTRAL SIDEBOARD ALCOVE

JERATHMAEL BOWERS HOUSE—1770—SOMERSET, MASSACHUSETTS

DINING ROOM END TOWARD FIREPLACE WITH ARCHED SIDE ALCOVES

feature, while at the same time maintaining separation of the rooms. An even more naive use is seen in the Jonathan Woodbridge house, built in a still more northern clime — in Hampshire County, Massachusetts—in 1806. Here the necessity for conserving heat during a large part of the year probably motivated the arrangement — which was obviously planned and built all at the same time; to separate a front from a rear hall, where the staircase was located off the rear hall space, and therefore the need for a practicable connection existed the year around.

In fact, it must by now have become apparent that the location of the archway in the hall is perhaps its most universal usage. In this location—midway the Hall's length — the archway is usually elliptical, and actually serves to focus interest upon the stairway, located behind it, that it thus visually enframes and emphasizes.

Among the considerable number of cross Hallway arches, were those in the Sarah Orne Jewett, Col. Isaac Royall, Jerathmael Bowers, and Capt. Gregory Purcell houses, along with the quite unique example from the Coleman-Hollister house. While the John Vassall House, in Cambridge, supplies still another example that, most unusually, springs from brackets on the

Courtesy Essex Institute

DOORWAY WITH ELLIPTICAL ARCHED TOPLIGHT

HOUSE AT 92 WASHINGTON
SQUARE, SALEM, MASS.

ARCHWAY TO PARLOR ALCOVE

side walls of the Hall that, in their turn, are set against the faces of small paneled pilasters extending from the floor.

Even more frequently, the arched top opening is found utilized in New England in a location under the upper run of the main stairway —or under its intermediate wide landing — thus providing both a special feature in the lower hallway and a partial support for the stairway construction thrown across above it. Instances of its use in this location have also been illustrated rather frequently within recent years, and another example, from the Saltonstall house; at Haverhill, Mass., is here shown as it appeared, both from the front hall as well as through the archway from the further entrance.

Besides this limited yet distinctive group, usually dating from the middle of the Eighteenth Century; with the beginning of the Century following, there appear a few smaller types that possess unusual charm and delicacy. Instead of springing across a wide central Hallway, at a location in front of the end hall staircase—these smaller archways are placed at the opening of side or intersecting corridors, that allowed them to be both narrower and smaller in scale than the more sturdy and wider-flung ones that had preceded them. While the former type actually often per-

ARCHED TOPLIGHT TO CLOSET
39-40 BEACON STREET—1818—
BOSTON, MASSACHUSETTS

formed a structural purpose, in concealing a heavy cross beam or tie, these later types are used almost exclusively for their decorative value; and the four examples, all attributed to Samuel McIntire, are those that have been used as models for most of the variants derived from them.

The use of arches upon each side of a central fireplace, to cover recessed alcoves, is also found in a few New England dwellings. Sometimes it is as simple and bold a treatment as in the 1780 portion of the Col. William R. Lee House at Marblehead where it is most unusually a full half-circle in outline; or, more usually, as an elliptical arch, in the example from an old Charlestown, Massachusetts, house that was in process of demolition even as these measurements were being taken, in 1934. In this instance, the same general treatment was employed in two separate parlors—in the one the archways framed recessed windows, and in the other, doorways. A still more ornate and elaborate treatment was employed in the West Parlor of the Vassall-Craigie - Longfellow house, 1759, at Cambridge, Mass., as well as in the Sargeant - Murray - Gilman - Hough house, 1768, at Gloucester, while the builders of the Royall House, at Medford, utilized similar—though sim-

ARCHED RECESS FORMERLY IN REAR PARLOR
AMORY-TICKNOR HOUSE—1804—BOSTON, MASS.

STAIRCASE HALL, SEEN THROUGH ARCHWAY FROM NORTH ENTRY

pler — motives on more than one of its floors.

In the Gloucester house a single circular headed window was placed directly in the center of the Hallway over the main stair landing. This employment was similar to that in the Sarah Orne Jewett House, at South Berwick, Maine, while, in a still more elaborate and decorative form, the best two examples in New England are in the Jeremiah Lee Mansion, at Marblehead and in "The Lindens," formerly at Danvers.

And still other uses for circular sash openings have been devised. To light an inner closet, a semicircular toplight, a circular window (or even an octagonal one!) can be employed. While, in plan, the slightly recessed niche with arched top, commonly used for a statuary figure, occurs in many hallways of the early Nineteenth Century.

STAIRCASE HALL AND ARCHWAY TO NORTH GARDEN ENTRANCE

HALL UNDER STAIR ARCHWAY, SALTONSTALL HOUSE— 1788—FORMERLY AT HAVERHILL, MASSACHUSETTS

ARCHED WALL CUPBOARD

ELISHA SMITH HOUSE—
STILLWATER, RHODE ISLAND

ARCHED DOUBLE DOORWAY

LEE-NICHOLS HOUSE—1660—
CAMBRIDGE, MASSACHUSETTS

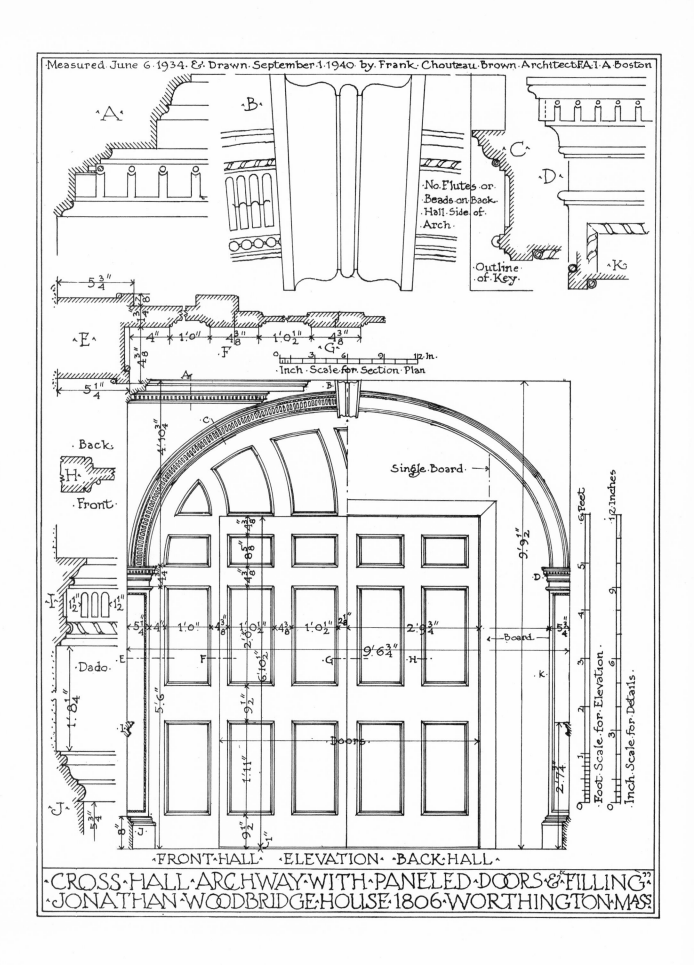

·Measured·June·6·1934·&·Drawn·September·1·1940·by·Frank·Chouteau·Brown·Architect·F.A.I.A·Boston·

·A·

·B·

·No.·Flutes·or·
Beads·on·Back·
Hall·Side·of·
Arch·

·C·

·D·

·Outline·
of·Key·

·K·

5 3/4"

3 3/8"
4 3/8"

·E·

4" 1'.0" 4 3/8" 1'.0 1/2" 4 3/8"

4 3/8"

·F·

·G·

0   3   6   9   12 In.
·Inch·Scale·for·Section·Plan·

5 1/4"

·A·

·B·

·Back·

·H·

·Front·

·C·

Single·Board·

4'.10 3/4"

9'.9 1/2"

·D·

·I·

1 1/2" 1 1/2"

·Dado·

4 3/4"

5 1/4" 4" 1'.0" 4 3/8" 1'.0 1/2" 4 3/8" 1'.0 1/2" 2 1/8"

2'.6 3/4"

5 3/4"

·Board·

2'.0 1/2"

6'.10 1/2"

9'.6 3/4"

1'.8 1/4"

·E·

·F·

·G·

·H·

·K·

5'.6"

9 1/2"

8 5/8"

4 3/8"

2'.7 1/4"

·Doors·

1'.11"

9 1/2"

8"

·J·

·C·

·L·

9 1/2"

1"

5 3/4"

·J·

6 Feet

5

4

3

2

1

·Foot·Scale·for·Elevation·

12 Inches

9

6

3

·Inch·Scale·for·Details·

·FRONT·HALL· ·ELEVATION· ·BACK·HALL·

·"CROSS·HALL·ARCHWAY·WITH·PANELED·DOORS·&·FILLING"·
·JONATHAN·WOODBRIDGE·HOUSE·1806·WORTHINGTON·MASS·

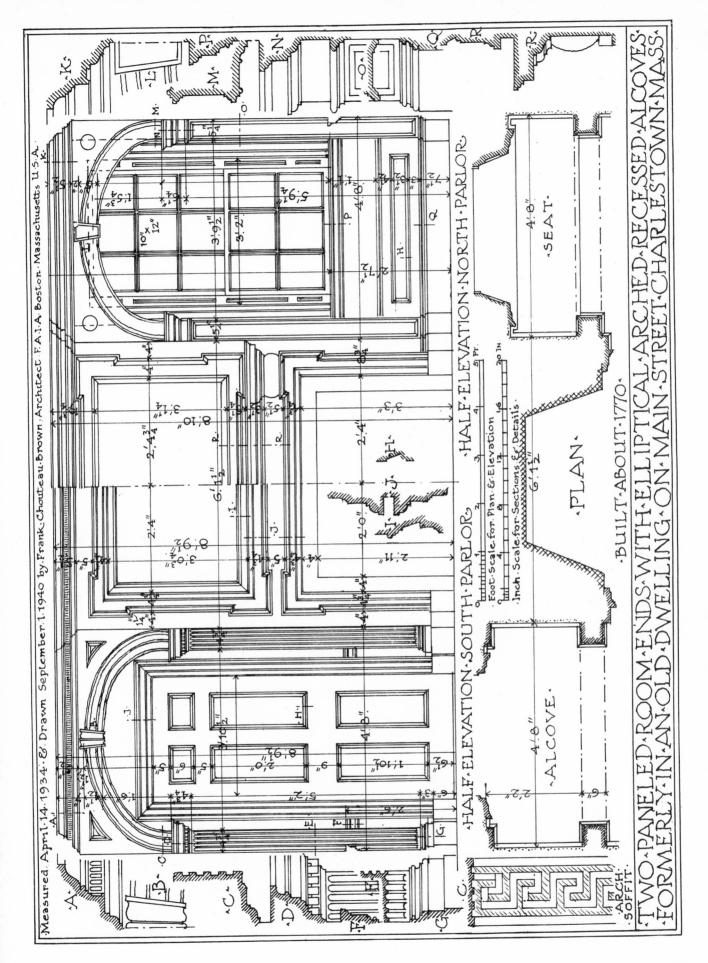

·TWO·PANELED·ROOM·ENDS·WITH·ELLIPTICAL·ARCHED·RECESSED·ALCOVES·
·FORMERLY·IN·AN·OLD·DWELLING·ON·MAIN·STREET·CHARLESTOWN·MASS·

·BUILT·ABOUT·1770·

·PLAN·

·HALF·ELEVATION·SOUTH·PARLOR·   ·HALF·ELEVATION·NORTH·PARLOR·

·SEAT·

·ALCOVE·

·ARCH·
·SOFFIT·

Foot·Scale·for·Plan·&·Elevation

Inch·Scale·for·Sections·&·Details

·Measured·April·14·1934·&·Drawn·September·1·1940·by·Frank·Chouteau·Brown·Architect·F·A·I·A·Boston·Massachusetts·U·S·A·

THE GARDNER-WHITE-PINGREE HOUSE
1804—SALEM, MASSACHUSETTS
Samuel McIntire, Architect

ARCHWAY, STAIRCASE HALL
TO FIRST FLOOR REAR ENTRY

VIEW THROUGH ARCHWAY
SECOND STORY STAIRCASE HALL

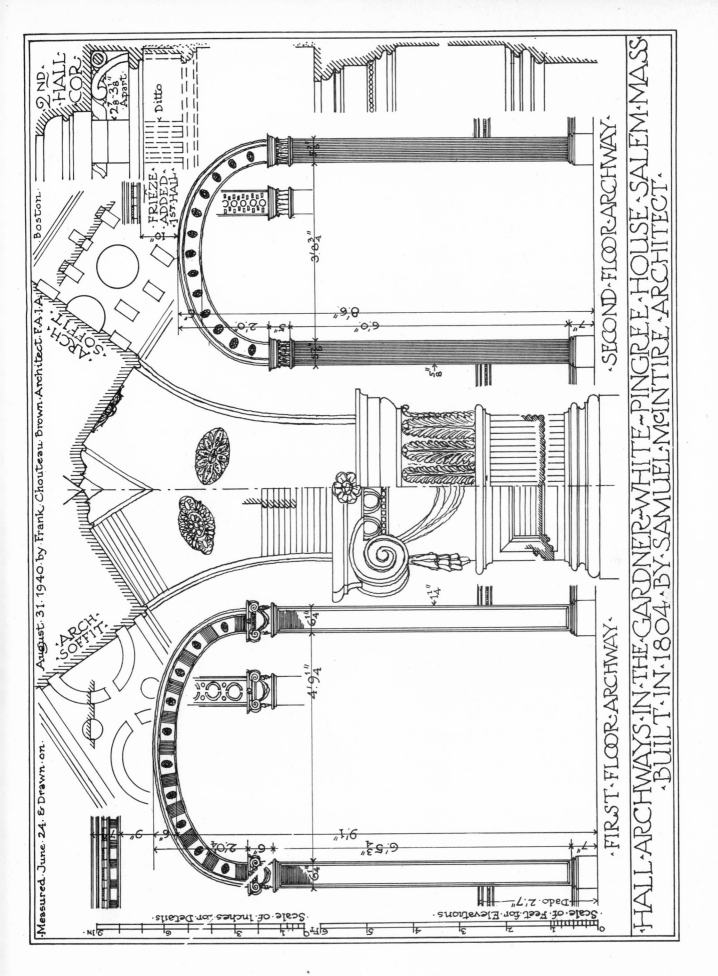

·HALL·ARCHWAYS·IN·THE·GARDNER~WHITE~PINGREE·HOUSE·SALEM·MASS·
·BUILT·IN·1804·BY·SAMUEL·McINTIRE·ARCHITECT·

·SECOND·FLOOR·ARCHWAY·

·FIRST·FLOOR·ARCHWAY·

·Measured·June·24·& Drawn·on·
·August·31·1940·by·Frank·Chouteau·Brown·Architect·F·A·I·A·
Boston·

2ND·
·HALL·
·COR·

·2'·8·38"·
Apart·

·FRIEZE·
·ADDED·
·1ST·HALL·

·ARCH·
·SOFFIT·

·ARCH·
·SOFFIT·

Ditto

Scale·of·Inches·for·Details·

Scale·of·Feet·for·Elevations·

183

ARCHES FORMERLY IN
EZEKIEL HERSEY DERBY HOUSE—
1799—SALEM, MASSACHUSETTS

Samuel McIntire, Architect

HALL ARCHWAYS IN ORIGINAL LOCATION,
BEFORE REMOVAL

FURTHER ARCH RELOCATED IN MCINTIRE
ROOM, PHILADELPHIA MUSEUM

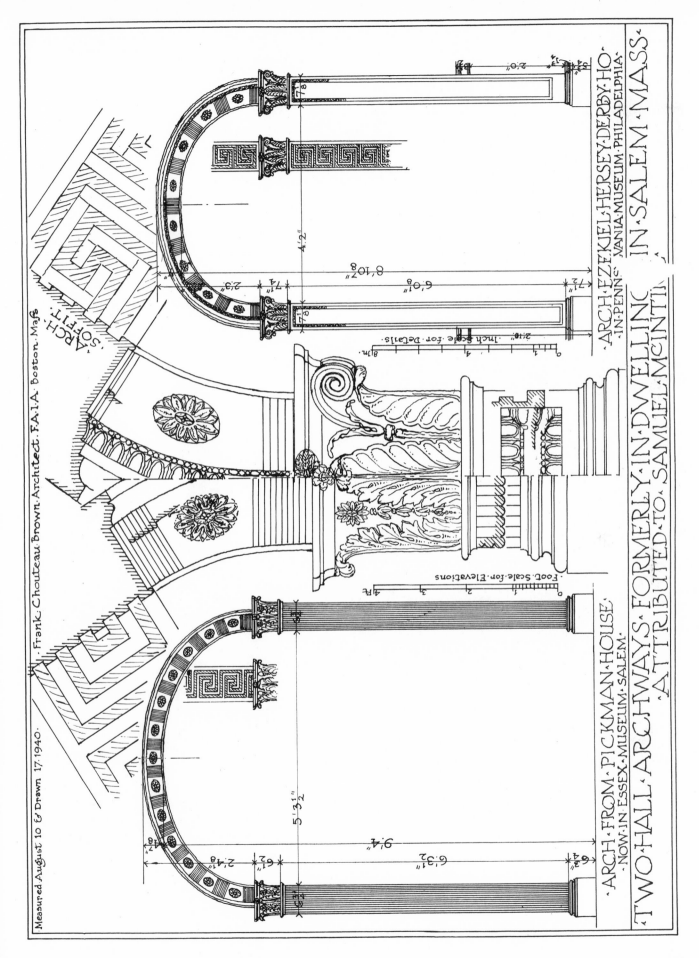

Measured August 10 & Drawn 17.1940.

·Frank·Chouteau·Brown·Architect·F·A·I·A·Boston·Mass·

·ARCH·SOFFIT·

·ARCH·FROM·PICKMAN·HOUSE·
·NOW·IN·ESSEX·MUSEUM·SALEM·

·ARCH·EZEKIEL·HERSEY·DERBY·HO·
·IN·PENN-SYLVANIA·MUSEUM·PHILADELPHIA·

·Inch·Scale·for·Details·

·Foot·Scale·for·Elevations·

·TWO·HALL·ARCHWAYS·FORMERLY·IN·DWELLING·IN·SALEM·MASS·
·ATTRIBUTED·TO·SAMUEL·McINTIRE·

DOORWAY IN MAIN HALL, COLEMAN-HOLLISTER HOUSE—1796—GREENFIELD, MASS.

Asher Benjamin, Architect

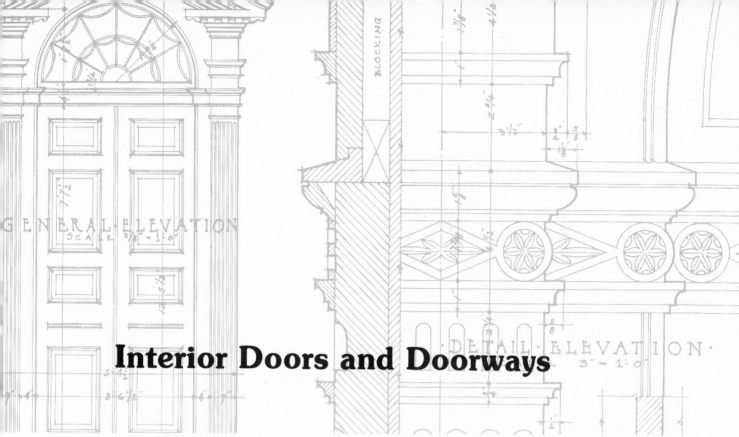

Interior Doors and Doorways

Especially vital in the architectural effect of interior doorways, is the method of "framing" or enclosing the door. In part, this may depend upon the structural method intended to "hang" the movable part of the design. The early "batten" door was hung with wrought iron strap hardware, placed against the face of the door, with iron nails driven through the cross batten upon the back, and "clinched" to make secure. The hinge was hung over a pin driven into the adjoining panel strip, of which the door's face was a part, or secured in a nearby post of the house frame. The "strike" of the door frame into which the panel swung was made as simply as by adding a two-inch strip across the top of the opening and two sides, against which the swinging panel would rest when closed.

The early development of a framed door, in northern New England, apparently "jumped" the transitional type that is found in great variety in early houses along the lower Hudson valley, and in parts of New Jersey and Pennsylvania. In New England, as elsewhere, the earliest doors were generally made of the same wide feather-edged boards as usually formed the inside wall of the first wooden dwellings built in this region. Sometimes it was made from a single piece of pine, twenty-six to thirty-four inches wide; sometimes of two or three pieces battened together upon the outer, or back, side of the opening. In the latter case, in New England, the wider board is placed most frequently in the center, and narrower pieces, apparently cut from the wider sections forming the wall on either side of the opening, complete the necessary width. In the Hudson Valley region, it is more

usual to find the center piece of the valve the narrowest, placed between two wider boards extending out to meet the sides of the door frame. In that region, too, this door is often set into a heavy interior masonry wall, instead of forming a part of a wooden partition along the inner room side. The cross "battens"—in New England usually two in number, and about four inches wide placed four to eight inches from the top and bottom of the door—are more frequently three in the Hudson Valley doors, where they are much wider and are often joined together with upright pieces strengthening the sides of the door, so that actually the effect of two panels is secured on what remains still, generally, the "back" of the door. The paneled effect is strengthened by the moulding that, more often than not, surrounds the inside of the space enclosed by these battens. In the prevalent "Dutch door" type, the wide center batten is split, so that half strengthens each part of the door.

In upper New England, at least, this "false paneled" effect is seldom found, although it appears to be a natural intermediate link between the plain batten and the framed and paneled door—so often of two panels only, in the earlier houses—almost all restricted to the early Eighteenth Century, or the few years immediately preceding it. In New England these early paneled examples are generally of genuinely framed and paneled workmanship, even though they are not over an inch in thickness.

Immediately following the batten "door," the opening was framed with two of the upright planks of the interior partition, which were finished on the sides toward the opening and rabbetted along that edge,

187

DOOR IN CAPT. SAMUEL TREVETT HOUSE—C1750
MARBLEHEAD, MASSACHUSETTS

DOOR IN THE GAY MANSE—C1795
SUFFIELD, CONNECTICUT

while a "header" or cross piece, similarly treated, was fitted in between these uprights to finish across the top of the opening. A raised moulding, or backband, was then broken or mitred around the whole frame about two to three inches back from the door, against which the plaster or paneling of the wall finished. A little later—early in the Nineteenth Century—the upright studs forming the wall construction were used only to enclose a rough opening, within which was set a heavier separate door frame, into which the door would fit. The latter was now heavier and thicker, and hung from hinges fastened into the rabbet, instead of on the face of the door frame. The space between the door and the rough construction of the partition was covered with a moulded façure board, of four to five inches width, and again backed with a heavier moulding,—which now covered the joint between plaster and wood, or made this separation between the materials more definite. It was first given a "bolection" type of surface outline,—and then shortly assumed its more customary later enframing section.

From this point onward the decorative advance was rapid. All sorts of fluted, carved, and moulded designs were employed upon the face of the applied finish treatment about the framed door opening. Pilasters were added at the sides, and frieze and cornices across the top to make an architectural cap or "overdoor"—to add grace, beauty and importance to the principal doorways within the better type of later Colonial dwelling.

Set within all this embellishment the door itself also was gradually becoming more varied in material and treatment. Sometimes walnut or mahogany were substituted for the simpler painted pine of earlier work. Sometimes both were combined, one for the stiles, the other for the panels. Sometimes the moulding separating the two was of still another material, such as ebony. And along with this the early years of the Nineteenth Century saw more panels added in height and width, in a greater variety of design and proportion. More elaborate panel moulds, of finer section, came into use and were often elaborately worked. The edge of the raised part of the panel developed its own moulded treatment. It was stopped, and then curved,—or broken at the corner angles. Or another edging mould was set in upon the face of the enclosed panel, and the space between was sometimes grooved or otherwise decoratively and appropriately treated.

At some time very soon after 1800 the moulding, that had formerly been run along the inner edges of the door stiles, was made separately, and the panel

DOOR IN PETER JAYNE HOUSE—C1724—
MARBLEHEAD, MASSACHUSETTS

DOOR IN THE MAJOR CHARLES FROST HOUSE—
C1730—EAST ELIOT, MAINE

was fitted into a groove in the stile edge, the moulding being added afterwards to hold the panel in place.

Then the double door was tried on the interior, to join—or to separate—two adjoining parlors, or a parlor from a wide hallway. At first it was hinged to swing, but it was soon arranged to slide back out-of-sight into the partition,—or to fold back into and become one of the sides of a paneled vestibule or alcove. For all of this, new and special types of hardware were employed, which would require another and separate article—all by itself.

Another unusual door is the partly-glazed door from the "King" Hooper House at Marblehead; and an example from the Peter Jayne House in the same town, displays a portion of the old stenciled border. In Marblehead and Danvers, stencils were used more in the form of borders, rather than in the all-over pattern shown in the Frost Farmhouse—just over the Maine border, at Eliot—that was popular in that region.

Turning to later and more decorative examples, the door and window from the Jerathmael Bowers House, in Somerset, shows a treatment derived partly, at least, from nearby Rhode Island influence, and of about thirty years later date than the dwelling itself. A stiff and heavy "overdoor" treatment appears in the Gen. Salem Towne House; while the door and doorhead from the Stevens-Tyler House in Andover, attributed to McIntire, is less graceful than his Salem work.

The Cook-Oliver House was built by Captain Samuel Cook in 1804, but some of its interior finish and the gateposts are believed to have been taken from the Elias Haskett Derby House, when it was demolished to make room for the Town House, several years later. A similar factor influenced the Peirce-Nichols House, which, although built in 1782, was not completed until 1801, when the eastern half shows a far more delicate McIntire treatment, including the carved doorheads.

Double-width doors, for interior locations, are not usual in Colonial work, but Salem provides us with a number of examples. Remembering its early Theatre, as well as its many early Ballrooms, connecting parlors, or wide hall openings met a social need, while means of closing them in winter were equally important.

Elaborate doorway treatments are found in the first Harrison Gray Otis House, by Charles Bulfinch, now headquarters of the Society for the Preservation of New England Antiquities. The variety of the cast putty ornaments—where the same detail is rarely repeated—appears with similar ornament in other mantels and details, near Boston.

DOOR IN THE RUGGLES-WOODBRIDGE HOUSE—1788
SOUTH HADLEY, MASSACHUSETTS

ORIGINAL GLAZED DOOR IN THE "KING" HOOPER
HOUSE—1745—MARBLEHEAD, MASSACHUSETTS

DOOR IN GEN. SALEM TOWNE HOUSE—
1796—CHARLTON, MASSACHUSETTS

DOORWAY IN STEVENS-TYLER HOUSE—C1800—
NORTH ANDOVER, MASSACHUSETTS

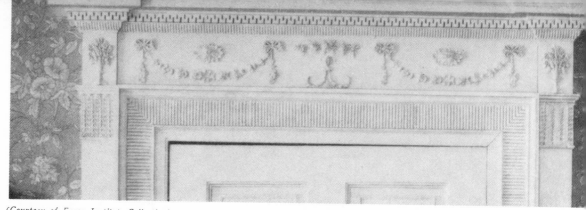

DOOR HEAD IN EAST PARLOR
PEIRCE-NICHOLS HOUSE—
1782—SALEM, MASSACHUSETTS
Samuel McIntire, Architect

DOOR HEAD IN ENTRANCE HALL
CUSTOM HOUSE—1819—SALEM, MASSACHUSETTS

LOOKING ACROSS ENTRANCE HALLWAY
(Showing Doors and Door Heads in Hall and Drawing Room)
GARDNER-WHITE-PINGREE HOUSE
SALEM, MASSACHUSETTS
Samuel McIntire, Architect

DOUBLE DOORWAY IN CAPT. EBENEZER
SHILLABER HOUSE—C1800—SALEM, MASS.

Samuel McIntire, Architect

DOUBLE DOORWAY,
FORMERLY IN JOSEPH PEABODY
HOUSE—1820—SALEM, MASSACHUSETTS

Samuel McIntire, Architect

HALL DOOR IN COOK-OLIVER HOUSE—
1804—SALEM, MASS.
SAMUEL McINTIRE, ARCHITECT

(Courtesy of Historic American Buildings Survey)
DOOR HEAD IN ENTRANCE HALL
COOK-OLIVER HOUSE—1804—SALEM, MASS.

194

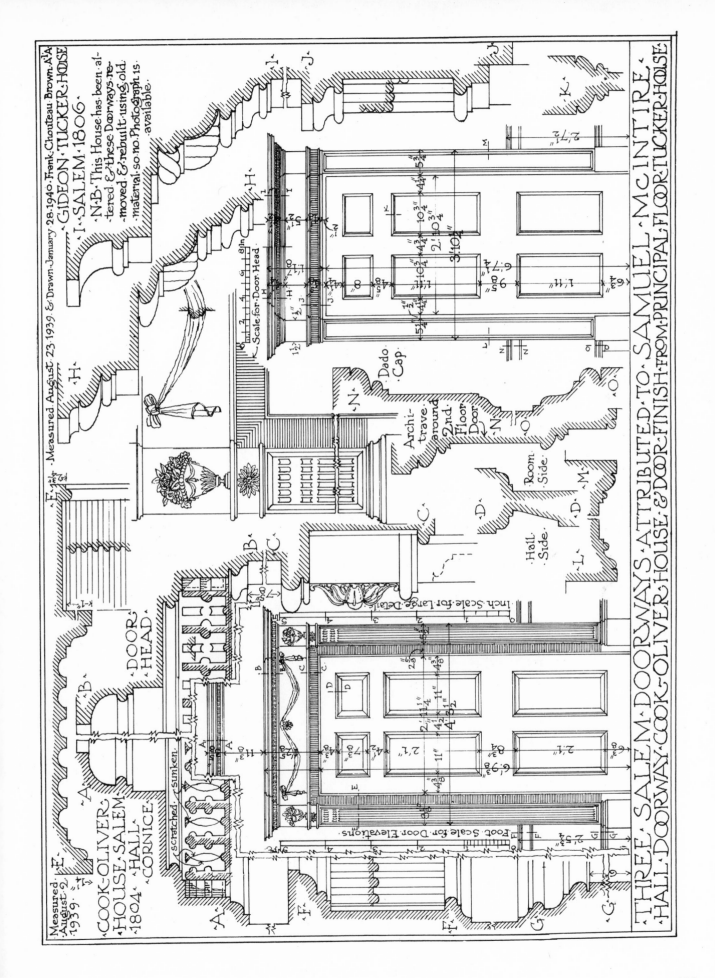

THREE·SALEM·DOORWAYS·ATTRIBUTED·TO·SAMUEL·MC INTIRE·
HALL·DOORWAY·COOK-OLIVER·HOUSE·&·DOOR·FINISH·FROM·PRINCIPAL·FLOOR·TUCKER·HOUSE·

·F· Measured·August·23·1939· & Drawn·January·28·1940· Frank·Chouteau·Brown·A.I.A.
·GIDEON·TUCKER·HOUSE·
·1·SALEM·1806·

N·B· This·House·has·been·al-
tered·&·these·Doorways·re-
moved·&·rebuilt·using·old·
material·so·no·Photograph·is·
available·

·Dado·
·Cap·

·Archi-
trave·
around·
2nd·
Floor·
Door·

·Room·
·Side·

·Hall·
·Side·

Inch·Scale·for·Large·Detail·

Scale·for·Door·Head·

Measured·
August·2·
1939·

·COOK-OLIVER·
·HOUSE·SALEM·
·1804· ·HALL·
·CORNICE·

·DOOR·
·HEAD·

scratched sunken·

Foot·Scale·for·Door·Elevations·

195

Doorways in
Corner of Dining
Room—FIRST
HARRISON GRAY
OTIS HOUSE—
1795—BOSTON,
MASSACHUSETTS
*Charles Bulfinch,
Architect*

196

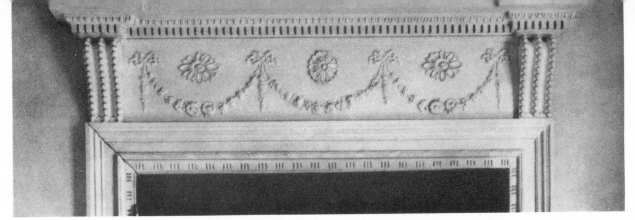

DOOR HEAD IN
DRAWING ROOM

DOORWAYS IN CORNER
OF DRAWING ROOM
FIRST HARRISON
GRAY OTIS HOUSE—
1795—BOSTON,
MASSACHUSETTS
Charles Bulfinch, Architect

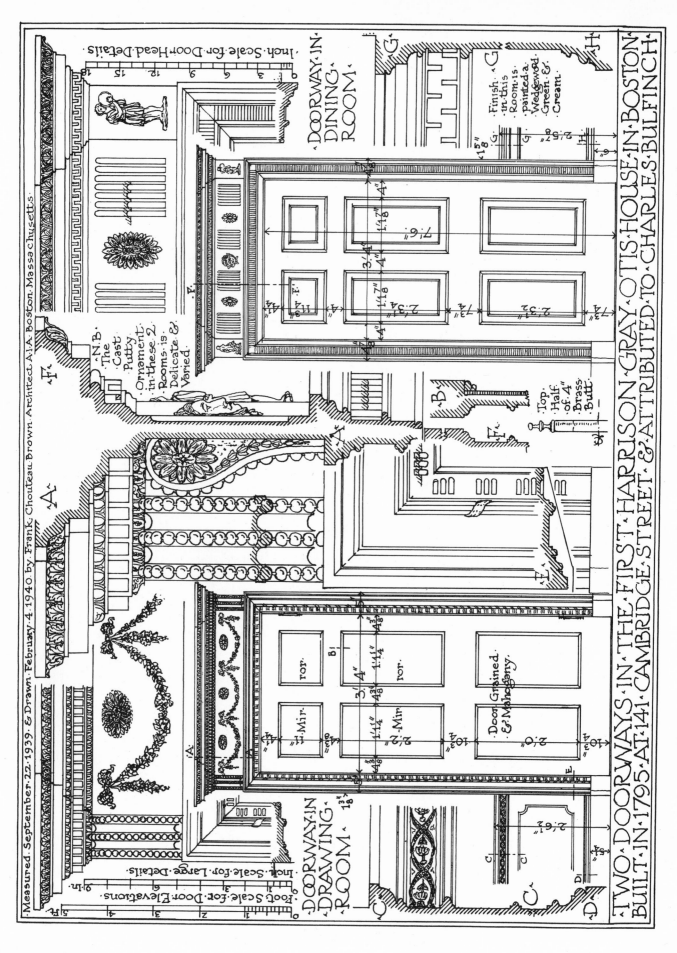

TWO·DOORWAYS·IN·THE·FIRST·HARRISON·GRAY·OTIS·HOUSE·IN·BOSTON·
BUILT·IN·1795·AT·141·CAMBRIDGE·STREET·&·ATTRIBUTED·TO·CHARLES·BULFINCH·

·DOORWAY·IN·DINING·ROOM·

·Finish·in·this·Room·is·painted·a·Wedgwood·Green·&·Cream·

·N.B.·The·Cast·Putty·Ornament·in·these·2·Rooms·is·Delicate·&·Varied·

·Top·Half·of·4"·Brass·Butt·

·Door·Grained·&·Mahogany·

·DOORWAY·IN·DRAWING·ROOM·

Inch·Scale·for·Door·Head·Details

Inch·Scale·for·Large·Details·
Foot·Scale·for·Door·Elevations·

Measured·September·22·1939·&·Drawn·February·4·1940·by·Frank·Chouteau·Brown·Architect·A.I.A·Boston·Massachusetts·

198

DOORWAY IN DINING ROOM, JARATHMAEL
BOWERS HOUSE—1770—SOMERSET, MASSACHUSETTS

Door Head in Ballroom

DOUBLE DOORWAY AT END
OF BALLROOM, OLD TOWN
HOUSE—1816—SALEM, MASSACHUSETTS
Samuel McIntire, Architect

GLOSSARY

ABACUS. The top member of the Doric capital. A flat rectangular slab, square in plan, it rests between the enchinus block of the capital and the lowest member of the entablature above.

ARCHITRAVE. The lowest member of a classical entablature. A molded lintel spanning between two columns.

BARGE BOARDS. An often ornamented board that conceals roof timbers projecting over gables.

BATTEN. A thin strip of lumber used especially to seal or reinforce a joint.

BELT COURSE. A narrow horizontal band of masonry which projects slightly from the wall. It is used primarily as a space divider.

BOLECTION MOULDING. That portion of a group of moldings which project beyond the general surface of a panel.

BRACKET. A supporting member projecting from the face of a wall to sustain a projecting ledge-like element, such as the eaves of a roof or a hood over a window, and frequently used for ornamental as well as for structural purposes.

CASEMENT WINDOWS. Windows that open from the side on hinges, like doors, out from the plane of the wall. Contrast with SASH WINDOWS.

CHAMFER. The oblique surface made by cutting off a square corner at an equal angle to each face.

COPING. The cap or top course of a wall, usually designed to shed water and often ornamental.

CORBEL. To build outward, by projecting successive courses of masonry beyond those below.

CORBELED CORNICE. A cornice made up of several projections each of which extends farther outward than the one below.

CORONA. The projecting part of a classic cornice.

CYMATIUM. The crowning member of a cornice generally in the form of a cyma, so called from its contour resembling that of a wave.

DADO. The lower part of an interior wall when especially decorated or faced; the decoration adorning this part of the wall.

DENTIL. A small ornamental block forming one of a series set in a row. A dentil molding is comprised of such a series.

DORMER WINDOW. A window in a sloping roof, with vertical sides and front.

ENGLISH BOND. Brick work in the colonies was laid in two methods, both traditional to English architecture. In English bond, the bricks are set in alternating courses of stretchers (bricks laid across the length of the wall with their long side showing) and headers (bricks laid across the wall with their short end showing); in Flemish bond the stretchers and headers alternate in the same row. This creates a more animated texture than English bond and was favored in the more elegant buildings.

ENTABLATURE. The top member of a classic order, being a richly molded continuous lintel supported on columns. It is divided horizontally into three main parts; the uppermost is the *cornice,* the middle one the *frieze,* and the lowest the *architrave.* Each has the moldings and decorative treatment that are characteristic of the particular order.

ENTASIS. A slight convexity of the shaft of the column.

ESCUTCHEONS. A protective or ornamental shield, as around a keyhole.

FACADE. An elevation or exterior front of a building, especially the principal or entrance front.

FASCIA. A flat horizontal member of an order or building having the form of a flat band.

FENESTRATION. The arrangement in a building of its windows, especially the more important and larger ones.

FESTOONS. A carved or molded ornament representing a festoon of flowers, fruits, or leaves, wound with a ribbon and hanging in a natural curve.

FINIAL. An ornament placed upon the apex of an architectural feature, such as a gable, turret, or canopy.

FLEMISH BOND. See ENGLISH BOND.

FRIEZE. Any long and narrow horizontal architectural member, especially one which has a chiefly decorative purpose. In Greek, Roman, and Neo-classical architecture it is that horizontal band which forms the central, and usually the most important, part of the entablature.

GABLE. A triangular-shaped piece of wall closing the end of a double pitched roof.

GAMBREL ROOF. A roof which has a double pitch. The lower place, which rises from the eaves, is rather steep; the upper plane, which spans from the lower to the ridgepole, has a flatter pitch.

GIRT. A principal horizontal beam in braced frame construction, such as chimney girt or end girt.

GUTTAE. One of a series of ornaments in the Doric entablature that is usually in the form of a frustrum of a cone.

HEADER. A brick laid with its end face to the weather. See ENGLISH BOND.

HIPPED ROOF. A roof which pitches inward from all four sides. The external angle formed where an end plane and side plane meet is called the hip.

JAMB. An upright surface forming the side of an opening as a door or a fireplace.

LINTEL. The horizontal structural member which supports the wall over an opening, or spans between two adjacent piers or columns.

METOPE. In a Doric entablature, that part of the frieze which falls between two triglyphs. In the Greek Doric order the metope characteristically contains sculpture.

MODILLION CORNICE. A cornice supported by a series of small ornamental brackets under the projecting top moldings. It is common to the Corinthian and Composite orders.

MORTISE AND TENON JOINT. A joint which is made by one member having its end cut in a projecting piece (tenon) which fits exactly into a groove or hole (mortise) in the other member. Once joined, the pieces are held together by a peg which passes through the tenon.

MULLION. An upright post or similar member dividing a window into two or more units, or lights, each of which may be further subdivided into panes.

MUNTINS. See MULLION

MUTULES. Projecting inclined blocks in the Doric cornices, derived from the ends of wooden beams.

ORDER. The most important elements of classical architecture are the orders, first developed as a structural-aesthetic system by the ancient Greeks. An order has two major components. A column with its capital forms the post, or main vertical supporting member. The principal horizontal member is the entablature, or lintel. The entablature consists of three horizontal parts. The lowest one is the architrave, an unbroken horizontal element which rests directly on the capitals and forms the principal part of the lintel. Above this is a second horizontal area called the frieze, which is generally decorated with sculptural ornament. The top member is the cornice; made up of various combinations of moldings, it overhangs the rest of the entablature and becomes the crowning motif. On the gabled end of a building, the cornice is continued up along the edge of the roof (now called a raking cornice) to form an enclosed triangle, or pediment. In classical architecture, the roof planes were pitched at a moderate angle, making the pediment a low, wide equilateral triangle. The Greeks developed three different types of orders, the Doric, Ionic, and Corinthian, each distinguishable by its own decorative system and proportions.

OVERHANG. The projection of an upper part of a building beyond the lower part.

PALLADIAN WINDOW. (sometimes called Palladian motif). An arrangement in which a round-headed window is flanked by lower square-headed openings and separated from them by columns or pilasters.

PEDIMENT. The low triangular gable formed by the roof slopes on top and the horizontal enclosing member, generally a cornice, beneath.

PILASTER. The projecting part of a square column which is attached to a wall; it is finished with the same cap and base as a freestanding column. Also a narrow vertical member in a similar position.

PLINTH. The lowest member of a base; a sub-base; a block upon which the moldings of an architrave or trim are stopped at the bottom.

PORTECOCHERE. A large gateway allowing vehicles to drive into a courtyard.

PORTICO. A porch consisting of a low-pitched roof supported on classical columns and finished in front with an entablature and pediment.

QUOIN. The bricks or stones laid in alternating directions, which bond and form the exterior corner angle of a wall.

RAIL. The vertical framing member which tenons into the stile.

RAKE. See ORDER.

REGULI. A short band, under the triglyphs of the Doric entablature, and to which the guttae are attached. (Generally, a surface that serves as a base for figures.)

RIDGEPOLE. The board or plank at the apex of a roof against which the upper ends of the rafters abut.

SASH WINDOWS. Windows with frames that slide vertically up and down in a grooved frame. In contrast with CASEMENT WINDOWS they open within the plane of the wall.

SKIRT. An apron piece or border, as a baseboard or the molded piece under a window stool.

SOFFIT. The underside of a subordinate part and member of buildings such as staircases, entablatures, archways, and cornices.

STILE. One of the upright pieces in framing or paneling; one of the primary members of a frame into which the rail tenons.

STRETCHER. A brick laid with its long face to the weather. See ENGLISH BOND.

SUMMER BEAM. In early New England braced frame construction, a large horizontal beam which runs from the chimney girt at right angles to the end girt in the outer frame, at a point opposite to the chimney.

TRANSOM. A horizontal bar, as distinguished from a mullion; especially one crossing a door or window opening near the top.

TRIGLYPH. One of the vertical blocks in a Doric frieze, suggesting, in stone, the outer ends of the ceiling beams that were used in primitive wooden construction. It has three narrow vertical elements which form two triangular channels.

TYMPANUM. The triangular wall of a pediment between its enclosing moldings, frequently ornamented with sculpture. The similarly placed wall over a square-headed door or window which is set in an arch.

VOUSSOIR. A wedge-shaped stone or brick used in the construction of an arch. Its taper toward the center is made to coincide with radii of the arch.

INDEX

INDEX TO ILLUSTRATIONS
AND MEASURED DRAWINGS